Building Forms with Vue.js

Patterns for building and scaling complex forms with great UX

Marina Mosti

BIRMINGHAM - MUMBAI

Building Forms with Vue.js

Copyright © 2019 Packt Publishing

All rights reserved. No part of this book may be reproduced, stored in a retrieval system, or transmitted in any form or by any means, without the prior written permission of the publisher, except in the case of brief quotations embedded in critical articles or reviews.

Every effort has been made in the preparation of this book to ensure the accuracy of the information presented. However, the information contained in this book is sold without warranty, either express or implied. Neither the author, nor Packt Publishing or its dealers and distributors, will be held liable for any damages caused or alleged to have been caused directly or indirectly by this book.

Packt Publishing has endeavored to provide trademark information about all of the companies and products mentioned in this book by the appropriate use of capitals. However, Packt Publishing cannot guarantee the accuracy of this information.

Commissioning Editor: Pavan Ramchandani
Acquisition Editor: Larissa Pinto
Content Development Editor: Aamir Ahmed
Senior Editor: Mohammed Yusuf Imaratwale
Technical Editor: Jane Dsouza
Copy Editor: Safis Editing
Project Coordinator: Manthan Patel
Proofreader: Safis Editing
Indexer: Tejal Daruwale Soni
Production Designer: Joshua Misquitta

First published: October 2019

Production reference: 1231019

Published by Packt Publishing Ltd.
Livery Place
35 Livery Street
Birmingham
B3 2PB, UK.

ISBN 978-1-83921-333-5

www.packt.com

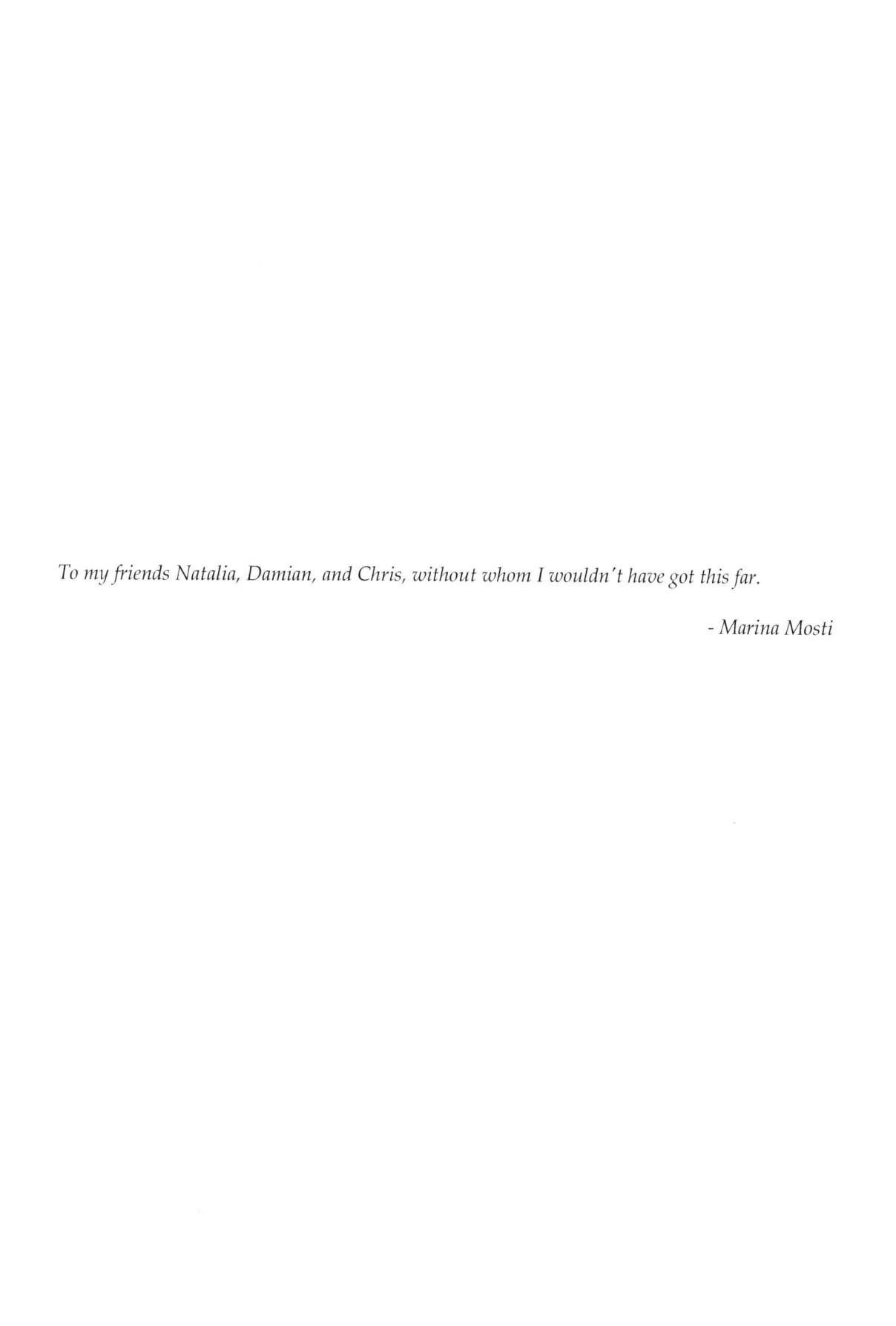

To my friends Natalia, Damian, and Chris, without whom I wouldn't have got this far.

- Marina Mosti

Packt.com

Subscribe to our online digital library for full access to over 7,000 books and videos, as well as industry leading tools to help you plan your personal development and advance your career. For more information, please visit our website.

Why subscribe?

- Spend less time learning and more time coding with practical eBooks and Videos from over 4,000 industry professionals

- Improve your learning with Skill Plans built especially for you

- Get a free eBook or video every month

- Fully searchable for easy access to vital information

- Copy and paste, print, and bookmark content

Did you know that Packt offers eBook versions of every book published, with PDF and ePub files available? You can upgrade to the eBook version at www.packt.com and as a print book customer, you are entitled to a discount on the eBook copy. Get in touch with us at customercare@packtpub.com for more details.

At www.packt.com, you can also read a collection of free technical articles, sign up for a range of free newsletters, and receive exclusive discounts and offers on Packt books and eBooks.

Foreword

I first became aware of Marina through her educational work, writing fun and accessible articles about Vue ranging from the very basics to advanced concepts such as object constancy and configuring Vue CLI. I later learned about her work on the Vuelidate team, building some of the most robust form libraries in the Vue ecosystem. Now I get to work with her directly as one of the first people I go to for help breaking down a difficult new concept for the Vue ecosystem.

I'm the one who recommended she write this book, as it's long overdue and she's the perfect person for the job. Building and maintaining complex forms in Vue is among the topics I get asked about the most, but comprehensive resources are still rare. Marina uses her expertise in this domain to provide the most approachable and complete introduction to the essential tools and strategies I've yet seen. It's a must-read for anyone who uses Vue, builds forms, and still has questions.

Chris Fritz, October 2019

Vue Team

Contributors

About the author

Marina Mosti is a full-stack web developer with over 13 years of experience in the field. She enjoys mentoring other women on JavaScript and her favorite framework, Vue, as well as writing articles and tutorials for the community.

She currently holds a position as Lead FE Developer at VoiceThread, and is the author of the FormVueLatte library as well as a member of the Vuelidate team. In her spare time, she enjoys playing bass, drums, and videogames.

About the reviewers

Natalia Tepluhina is a Vue.js core team member and a Senior Frontend Engineer at GitLab. She is a conference speaker and author of articles on different topics related to Vue.js. Thanks to these activities, Natalia has got the title of Google Developer Expert in Web Technologies.

Chris Fritz is an educator/developer hybrid and consultant who draws on his upbringing as a cultural mutt to help Vue devs around the world be happier in their work. He's most well known for his work on the Vue docs and Vue Enterprise Boilerplate, as well as speaking, leading workshops, and cohosting a weekly podcast called Views on Vue. When he's not working, he's probably reading speculative fiction, working out with lightsabers in virtual reality, frowning at puzzle games while he insists he's having fun—or even outside enjoying a hike with friends.

Packt is searching for authors like you

If you're interested in becoming an author for Packt, please visit `authors.packtpub.com` and apply today. We have worked with thousands of developers and tech professionals, just like you, to help them share their insight with the global tech community. You can make a general application, apply for a specific hot topic that we are recruiting an author for, or submit your own idea.

Table of Contents

Preface — 1

Chapter 1: Setting up the Demo Project — 7
- Technical requirements — 7
- Installing Vue CLI onto our computer — 8
- Creating our new project — 10
- A quick look at the project structure — 12
- Summary — 13

Chapter 2: A Form in its Simplest Form — 15
- Technical requirements — 15
- Getting started using Bootstrap — 16
- Actually writing some code — 17
- Binding the inputs to local state — 18
- Submitting the form's data — 21
- Bringing in Axios — 22
- Summary — 24

Chapter 3: Creating Reusable Form Components — 25
- Technical requirements — 26
- Breaking down the form into components — 26
- Understanding v-model in custom components — 29
- Implementing a custom input component — 31
- One more time – with dropdowns! — 34
- Summary — 39

Chapter 4: Input Masks with v-mask — 41
- Technical requirements — 41
- Installing the v-mask library — 42
- Exploring the v-mask directive — 43
- Enhancing our custom inputs — 44
- Summary — 45

Chapter 5: Input Validation with Vuelidate — 47
- Technical requirements — 47
- Installing dependencies — 48
- Creating validation rules — 48
- Moving validation into our custom inputs — 52
- Adding the final touches — 56
- Summary — 58

Chapter 6: Moving to a Global State with Vuex — 59
Technical requirements — 60
Adding Vuex to our project — 60
Creating the mock API endpoint — 61
Creating the global state — 64
Adding some mutations to our store — 66
Lights, Vue, actions! — 66
Vuelidate and Vuex — 69
Summary — 73

Chapter 7: Creating Schema-Driven Forms — 75
Technical requirements — 76
Exploring the starter kit — 76
Preparing the schema — 77
    Loading the schema and creating a Renderer component — 78
Dynamically binding the user's data — 81
Creating a mock API — 84
Loading the new API into the app — 86
Translating the API into a working schema — 87
Summary — 89

Other Books You May Enjoy — 91

Index — 95

Preface

Vue.js is one of the world's leading and fastest growing frameworks for frontend development. Its gentle learning curve and vibrant and helpful community have made it an easy choice for many new developers looking to harness the power of frontend frameworks. Additionally, its flexibility and power have made it an easy choice for advanced developers and companies to use it as their main tool for powerful, dynamic, and lean applications and websites.

In *Building Forms with Vue.js*, we will explore a specific part of frontend development—forms. We will journey together, from creating the most basic forms all the way through to understanding how a fully dynamic, schema-driven form works.

Who this book is for

Building Forms with Vue.js is aimed at frontend developers who have a basic understanding of the Vue.js framework and who want to understand how to better create powerful and reusable forms.

What this book covers

`Chapter 1`, *Setting up the Demo Project*, will guide you through setting up the base of the project that we will be building on throughout the book. It is recommended that you work through the book in the order of the chapters, as they build on the concepts learned in the previous ones. However, the completed code for each chapter will be provided at the beginning of each in case you want to skip forward.

`Chapter 2`, *A Form in its Simplest Form*, shows the basics of building a basic web form, and the process of connecting the inputs to your app's state. You will also learn about the basics of submitting the form, and using the Axios library to make asynchronous calls to the backend.

`Chapter 3`, *Creating Reusable Form Components*, will teach you how to break down a form into components that can be reused throughout your application. You will understand how the `v-model` directive works and how the main application and form can leverage these components.

Preface

Chapter 4, *Input Masks with v-mask*, touches upon using the `v-mask` library to allow for input masking to improve user experience. You will learn how to implement third-party plugins and how to incorporate them into your custom components.

Chapter 5, *Input Validation with Vuelidate*, walks you through the process of adding Vuelidate—a powerful form validation library—to your project, creating validation rules and applying them to your form, as well as how to incorporate it into your custom components.

Chapter 6, *Moving to a Global State with Vuex*, takes things a step further by transferring the current application's local state to a global state by leveraging the power of Vuex—the official global state management library and pattern. We will incorporate Vuelidate and our custom components into the mix.

Chapter 7, *Creating Schema-Driven Forms*, brings all the previous concepts together and walks you through the process of understanding and creating a renderer component that allows your application to be fully schema-driven. It will react to API changes provided by a mock API, as well as provide an explanation of how to generate a fully constructed form complete with data submission to the mock backend.

To get the most out of this book

In order for you to follow this book easily, I have to make some assumptions regarding some pre-existing knowledge on your end. Here's a checklist of the basic requirements you need in order to get the most out of this book:

- You have used HTML, CSS, and JavaScript before and are comfortable creating basic web applications.
- You are familiar with `console.log` statements and the general debugging of web apps in a browser such as Chrome.
- Basic knowledge of Terminal commands. You should know how to navigate folders with the `cd` command at the very least.
- You understand basic concepts of Vue, such as state, reactivity, interpolation, computed properties, and methods. Make sure that you take a look at the **Essentials** part of the official guide for reference: https://vuejs.org/v2/guide/.
- You have access to a computer and an internet connection to download and install the required libraries and project files.

In the first chapter of this book, we will go over how to set up your project with an easy-to-follow step list.

Download the example code files

You can download the example code files for this book from your account at `www.packt.com`. If you purchased this book elsewhere, you can visit `www.packtpub.com/support` and register to have the files emailed directly to you.

You can download the code files by following these steps:

1. Log in or register at `www.packt.com`.
2. Select the **Support** tab.
3. Click on **Code Downloads**.
4. Enter the name of the book in the **Search** box and follow the onscreen instructions.

Once the file is downloaded, please make sure that you unzip or extract the folder using the latest version of:

- WinRAR/7-Zip for Windows
- Zipeg/iZip/UnRarX for Mac
- 7-Zip/PeaZip for Linux

The code bundle for the book is also hosted on GitHub at `https://github.com/PacktPublishing/Building-Forms-with-Vue.js`. In case there's an update to the code, it will be updated on the existing GitHub repository.

We also have other code bundles from our rich catalog of books and videos available at `https://github.com/PacktPublishing/`. Check them out!

Download the color images

We also provide a PDF file that has color images of the screenshots/diagrams used in this book. You can download it here: `https://static.packt-cdn.com/downloads/9781839213335_ColorImages.pdf`.

Code in Action

Visit the following link to check out videos of the code being run:

`http://bit.ly/2puBGN1`

Preface

Conventions used

There are a number of text conventions used throughout this book.

`CodeInText`: Indicates code words in text, database table names, folder names, filenames, file extensions, pathnames, dummy URLs, user input, and Twitter handles. Here is an example: "Let's get started with the installation of the `v-mask` library."

A block of code is set as follows:

```
<input
 type="text"
 v-model="form.telephone"
 v-mask="'(###)###-####'"
>
```

Any command-line input or output is written as follows:

```
> npm install v-mask
```

Bold: Indicates a new term, an important word, or words that you see on screen. For example, words in menus or dialog boxes appear in the text like this. Here is an example: "Go back to the first tab, **Response & Body**."

Warnings or important notes appear like this.

Tips and tricks appear like this.

Get in touch

Feedback from our readers is always welcome.

General feedback: If you have questions about any aspect of this book, mention the book title in the subject of your message and email us at customercare@packtpub.com.

Errata: Although we have taken every care to ensure the accuracy of our content, mistakes do happen. If you have found a mistake in this book, we would be grateful if you would report this to us. Please visit www.packtpub.com/support/errata, selecting your book, clicking on the Errata Submission Form link, and entering the details.

Piracy: If you come across any illegal copies of our works in any form on the internet, we would be grateful if you would provide us with the location address or website name. Please contact us at copyright@packt.com with a link to the material.

If you are interested in becoming an author: If there is a topic that you have expertise in, and you are interested in either writing or contributing to a book, please visit authors.packtpub.com.

Reviews

Please leave a review. Once you have read and used this book, why not leave a review on the site that you purchased it from? Potential readers can then see and use your unbiased opinion to make purchase decisions, we at Packt can understand what you think about our products, and our authors can see your feedback on their book. Thank you!

For more information about Packt, please visit packt.com.

Setting up the Demo Project

Every great app ever deployed began as a single line of code, and with a long road ahead of us, we should start, as they say, at the beginning.

We will be using Vue CLI 3 in this book to set up our project structure. Vue CLI is an amazing tool to quickly scaffold Vue applications. Vue CLI was born to be the go-to tool for scaffolding applications. Even though there are other amazing solutions, such as Nuxt, knowing the basics of Vue CLI will get you going with most projects. If you haven't used it before, don't worry: we will dive into the setup step by step together.

In this chapter, we will cover the following topics:

- Installing Vue CLI onto our computer
- Creating our new project
- A quick look at the project structure

Technical requirements

The following are the requirements for this chapter:

- You will need a computer with access to a Terminal program such as Apple's Terminal or Windows' Command Prompt.
- Node version 8.9 or above and **Node Package Manager** (**npm**): installation instructions will be provided in this chapter.
- You will need an **Integrated Development Environment** (**IDE**) of your preference. A great free one can be found at `https://code.visualstudio.com/`

Setting up the Demo Project

The code files for this chapter can be found in the following GitHub repository:

`https://github.com/PacktPublishing/Building-Forms-with-Vue.js/tree/master/Chapter01`.

Check out the following video to see the code in action:

`http://bit.ly/2OXLxpg`

Installing Vue CLI onto our computer

At the time of writing, the Vue CLI has the requirements of Node version 8.9 or above (8.11.0+ is recommended), so we need to make sure you have that set up on your development computer first.

To check if you already have it installed, perform the following steps:

1. Open up a Terminal (also known as a command line!)
2. Execute the `node -v` command

If you get back an output with a version tag, then you have it installed, and you can skip ahead.

If you don't have Node already, head over to the following link in your browser: `nodejs.org`.

You should be presented with a **Home** screen and two big green download buttons. We will be using the one labeled **Current**, as shown in the following screenshot:

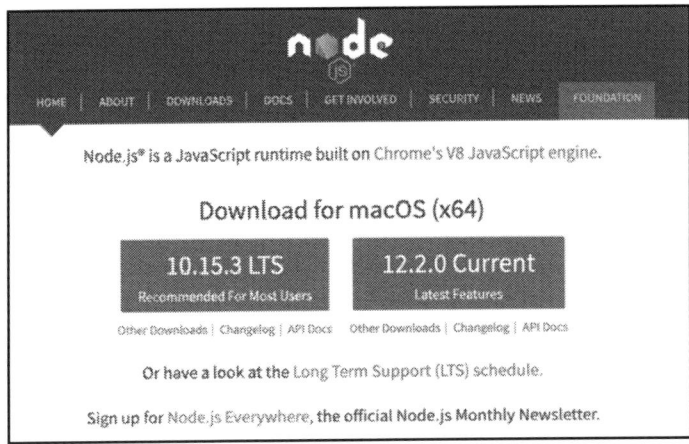

[8]

So, go ahead and click on the button and follow the installation instructions for your own OS.

Once the installation is complete, verify that everything is working correctly:

1. Open your Terminal
2. Execute the `node -v` command

You should get an output similar to **v12.2.0**, verifying that the node has correctly been installed to your system.

To actually get Vue CLI installed to our system, however, we still need to make use of a package manager.

Now, when you installed Node, you actually got a copy of `npm` installed on your system for free. You can verify this by typing `npm -v` in your Terminal, and, as before, you will get a version number as output.

Be aware that the Vue CLI requires Node version 8.9 or above (8.11.0+ recommended) at the time of writing, but make sure you check the following link for the exact version number for the moment you follow this book: `vuejs.org/guide/installation.html`.

Finally, it is time to actually get things up and running. Fire up your Terminal once again, and run the following command:

```
> npm install --global @vue/cli
```

The Terminal will go ahead and download all of the required files onto your computer and set them up in a globally accessible path so you can use this CLI tool anywhere on your computer. Neat, right?

Note the `--global` flag on this command. What this means is that you're installing this package globally on your computer. In short, this means that you will be able to use the commands from anywhere inside your filesystem, without having to navigate to a specific folder.

For future reference, you can also use the shorthand for `--global`, which is simply `-g`.

Once more, let's check that everything was installed properly by running `vue --version` on the Terminal. You should get back the version number of Vue CLI.

Now that we have our CLI set up, we can start with creating our new project. Let's dive deeper into how to do this in the following section.

Setting up the Demo Project

Creating our new project

Navigate into a folder of your choice that will hold your project files. Don't worry—we don't need to set up servers, virtual hosts, or anything of that sort. The Vue CLI will actually set up a development server for us every time we run our project's scripts, so you can create it wherever you prefer.

The command you want to run now is `vue create <name>`, where `<name>` is the name of your project—and the folder that will be created.

We will create our new project by running the following:

```
> vue create vuetiful-forms
```

The `vuetiful-forms` part of the command will name the project folder. Feel free, of course, to name it as you best see fit.

Once you run this command, the Vue CLI will display a wizard that will let you configure the way you want your project to be set up:

```
2. vue create vuetiful-forms (node)
Vue CLI v3.7.0
? Please pick a preset: (Use arrow keys)
> SPA-default (vue-router, vuex, node-sass, babel, eslint, unit-mocha)
  default (babel, eslint)
  Manually select features
```

We will go ahead and select **Manually select features** as we want to play around and see what options we can toggle on and off. Please be aware that the decisions we make here are not final. Anything can be added or removed later on, so don't worry!

The first screen presents us with different features and packages that we can choose:

1. Select **Babel** and **Lint/Formatter**, which are the default two options. Later on in this book, we will add Vuex to our project manually.
2. Hit the spacebar to select any options and the *Enter* key to proceed to the next screen.
3. In the **linter/formatter** configuration screen, use the **ESLint with error prevention only** configuration.
4. On the next screen, we will pick **Lint on save**. (Feel free to pick the other option if you don't like auto-linting.)

5. For our configuration, choose to store it **In dedicated config files** to keep our `package.json` file as neat as possible.
6. Finally, you can **Save this as a preset for future projects** if you would like to do so.

As a side note, please be aware that, depending on the choices you make, you may be presented with different configurations than the ones I have explained here.

The Terminal will once again go to work, and behind the scenes, it will create the project structure for your new project:

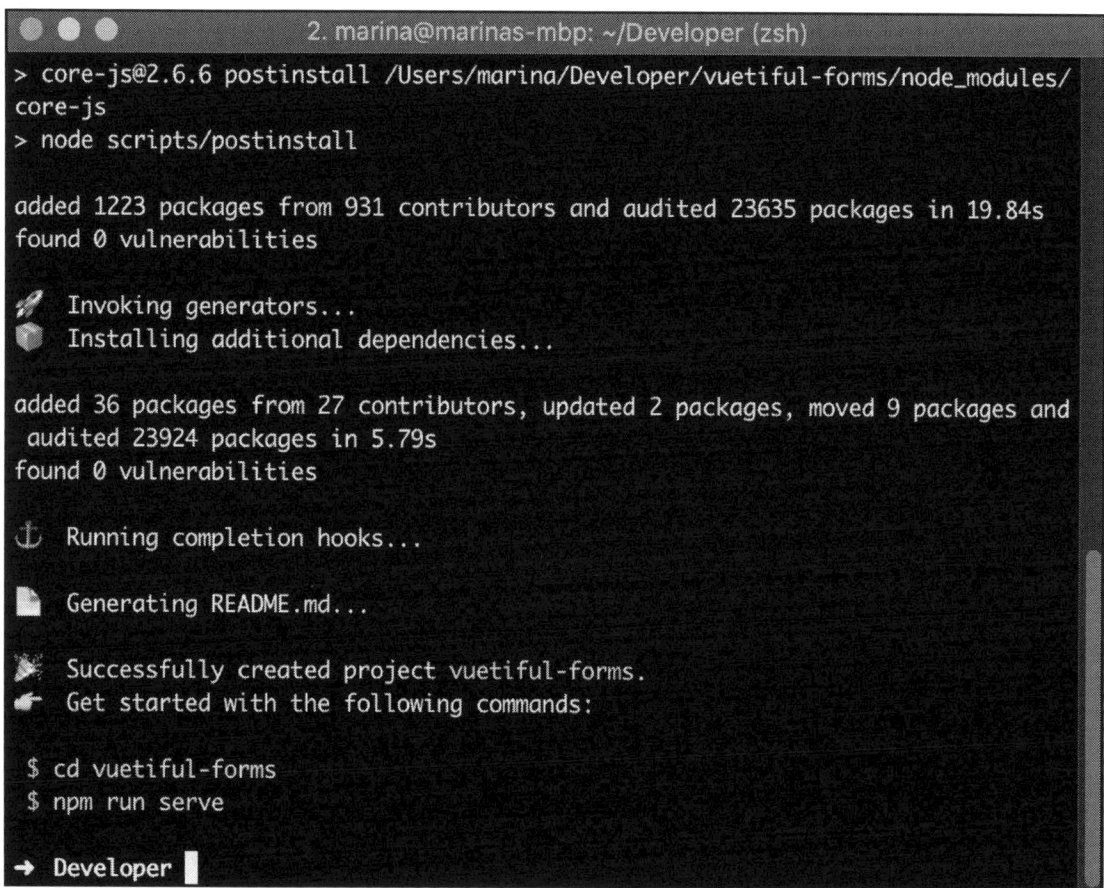

With this easy-to-follow wizard, you can easily scaffold all of your projects, but don't worry if you didn't select a particular option during this phase; the Vue CLI makes it super easy to add and remove plugins later on! Let's take a quick look at our project now.

A quick look at the project structure

Go ahead and open your new `vuetiful-forms` folder in your favorite code editor. If you don't already have an IDE for development, you can get a really good one for free from `code.visualstudio.com`.

Your project structure will look like the following screenshot:

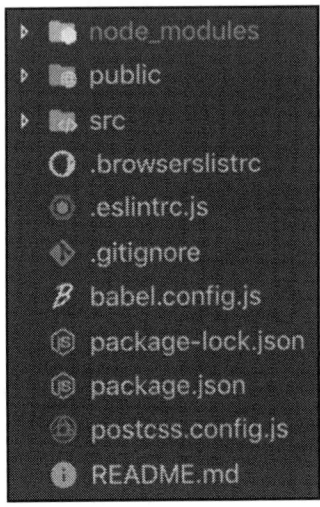

Here is a quick rundown of what you can find inside the structure:

- **node_modules**: This holds your dependencies—the code packages that you can install or remove using `npm`.
- **public**: This folder will hold `index.html`, which your web server will load up when you navigate to the app's URL. All of the files that it will need will be auto-injected by Vue, so you don't need to worry about what happens here.
- **src**: This is where you will put all of your code, components, assets, and so on.

On your project root, you will see a configuration file like `.eslintrc.js` for your ESLint configuration, `.gitignore` for Git, your `package.json` and `package-lock.json` or `yarn.lock` files for package management, and others depending on your previous choices.

These files are used for changing preferences on each one of these services and can be safely ignored if you don't have experience tweaking them.

Summary

At this point, you know all of the basics of scaffolding a Vue CLI-powered application and have had your first glimpse of the project structure.

In the next chapter, we will get our project up and running, and we will start working on actual forms!

2
A Form in its Simplest Form

All right! Let's dive into this headfirst (with a little detour on the way to make it look pretty). We will create a very simple page with a form. This form will ask for some basic personal data from our user, and the second part of the form will be used for more specific questions.

By the end of this chapter, you will have a solid understanding of how to build basic forms in Vue, plus you'll get a quick refresher on basic Vue concepts such as `v-model`, events, and properties.

In this chapter, we will cover the following topics:

- Getting started using Bootstrap
- Actually writing some code
- Binding the inputs to local state
- Submitting the form's data
- Bringing in Axios

Technical requirements

The code for this chapter can be found in the following GitHub repository:

https://github.com/PacktPublishing/Building-Forms-with-Vue.js/tree/master/Chapter02.

A Form in its Simplest Form

Check out the following video to see the code in action:

`http://bit.ly/35F6340`

Getting started using Bootstrap

Let's begin by adding Bootstrap 4 as a dependency to our project, so we won't have to think about design and can focus on the functionality of our forms.

Bootstrap is a popular open source toolkit that gives us some predefined classes and styles so that we can make our app look nice without having to worry much about styles.

To get Bootstrap installed and set up for our project, follow these steps:

1. Open up the Terminal to your project's folder, and install the dependency with the following command:

   ```
   > npm install bootstrap
   ```

2. Awesome! This adds the package to our `node_modules` folder and `package.json`. Now, go ahead and import the necessary styles into `src/main.js`. Use the following command to do so:

   ```
   import 'bootstrap/dist/css/bootstrap.min.css';
   ```

We're not going to be using any of Bootstrap's scripts, so we can live with only the minified CSS.

Let's do a little cleaning on our `App.vue` file because, right now, we only have some boilerplate code—but we want to start fresh! So, let's begin the cleaning:

1. Replace everything inside `App.vue` with the following code:

   ```
   <template>
     <div id="app">
     </div>
   </template>

   <script>
   export default {
     name: 'app'
   }
   </script>
   ```

2. Go ahead and start up your development server by running the following on your Terminal:

   ```
   > npm run serve
   ```

3. Open up the link that the Terminal shows you (the one that says **local**) and you should see a blank screen in your browser.

Behold the blank canvas of the first steps to form greatness and stuff! Yaaas!

Let's move on and get working on the actual form. It's time for some code.

Actually writing some code

All right, enough setup—let's write some code! We will start with a very simple form so that our users can fill out their personal information. Nothing crazy, just baby steps.

We are going to add three fields to our form. A `firstName` input, a `lastName` input, and an `email` input. Finally, we will add a `Submit` button.

Remember back when we installed Bootstrap? This is where it comes out to shine. All of the classes that we are going to add to our markup will get magically styled by Bootstrap.

Make these changes to your `App.vue` file:

```
<template>
  <div id="app" class="container py-4">
    <div class="row">
      <div class="col-12">
        <form>
          <div class="form-group">
            <label>First Name:</label>
            <input type="text" class="form-control">
          </div>

          <div class="form-group">
            <label>Last Name:</label>
            <input type="text" class="form-control">
          </div>

          <div class="form-group">
            <label>Email:</label>
            <input type="email" class="form-control">
          </div>
```

```
            <div class="form-group">
              <button type="submit" class="btn btn-primary">Submit</button>
            </div>
          </form>
        </div>
      </div>
    </div>
</template>
```

In the previous code example, we have set up a container with `row`. Inside this `row`, we have populated it with three different inputs, two `text` types (one for the first and one for the last name), and an `email` type input. Finally, we added `<button>`, which will serve as the main way to submit the form.

Save your file and check out your browser. If you still have the server running, you should see the changes reflected automatically. Okay, I agree it's a little underwhelming, but I did say we're starting with a simple example, and this is as simple as it gets!

The form is fully functional, and you can even click the **Submit** button for it to submit to itself and accomplish absolutely nothing. Neat! But let's spice this up with some Vue.

Binding the inputs to local state

The purpose of forms in a web application is to capture some user input and be able to do something with it. In our example, we still don't have any way to access the user's input with JavaScript for our Vuetiful plans—so, let's start with that.

Please note that you do not necessarily have to wrap up your form's data inside a secondary object, but, I have found it to be cleaner—especially when you start adding other data properties to your component, which may not necessarily be related to your form.

Create a new `data` property on the instance of your `App.vue` file. Inside of it, we're going to declare a `form` object, which will, in turn, hold a property for each one of our inputs:

```
<script>
export default {
  name: 'app',
  data() {
    return {
      form: {
        firstName: '',
        lastName: '',
        email: ''
      }
```

```
      }
    }
  }
</script>
```

For us to bind our inputs' values to our internal state, we need to make use of Vue's `v-model` attribute. So, let's add `v-model` to each of our inputs. That way, whenever the user types in or deletes information, the value of the input element will be bound to our `data` property.

Remember that `v-model` is not a *magical* attribute. It is a shorthand for two things:

- It binds the `input` event of our input boxes:

  ```
  v-on:input="form.name = $event.target.value"
  ```

- It binds the `value` attribute to our `data` property:

  ```
  v-bind:value="form.firstName"
  ```

Go ahead and add `v-model` to all of our inputs:

```
...
<div class="form-group">
  <label>First Name:</label>
  <input
    v-model="form.firstName"
    type="text"
    class="form-control"
  >
</div>
<div class="form-group">
  <label>Last Name:</label>
  <input
    v-model="form.lastName"
    type="text"
    class="form-control"
  >
</div>
<div class="form-group">
  <label>Email:</label>
  <input
    v-model="form.email"
    type="email"
    class="form-control"
  >
</div>
```

A Form in its Simplest Form

The following screenshot shows the Vue developer tools displaying the two-way data binding between our form and the internal state in our data:

Great job! Now, this isn't super impressive, but we are building the foundations for things to come.

In the following section, we're going to look at how to handle the form being submitted and sent to an API endpoint.

Submitting the form's data

As it currently is, the form is getting submitted to the same URL when you click the **Submit** button. This is not Vue magic—this is just default `<form>` behavior, especially since we didn't specify an action attribute on the tag.

In most real-world scenarios, you'll want to perform a couple of operations before submitting a form. The most common would be validating some inputs, or perhaps even overriding the default submit behavior with an asynchronous call using a library such as Axios.

First, we need to make sure that, when the user clicks the **Submit** button, we prevent the form from going out on its own. We also want to bind a new method to it being clicked.

Let's bind to the form's `submit` event first. Remember that we want to add the `.prevent` modifier to the event so that, when the form is submitted, the default behavior doesn't trigger, and our function will run as expected:

```
<form @submit.prevent="onSubmit">
  ...
</form>
```

Sweet! Now we need to create this new `onSubmit` method on the configuration of our `App.vue` file. Let's use `console.log` inside the `click` method handler to verify that it works before going into more detail.

Add this code as a property inside the export default declaration:

```
methods: {
  onSubmit() {
    console.log('click');
  }
}
```

Just to verify that everything is working, go ahead and open up your browser and click the **Submit** button a few times. Check the console; the log should say **click**. So far, so good—we've managed to take control of the form's behavior.

Let's make a *very* basic validation method as an example. We will verify that the input's length is > 0 (not empty) for the three fields. In a later chapter, we will go into Vuelidate, which will provide more deep and powerful validation to our forms.

A Form in its Simplest Form

Let's make a new computed property called `formIsValid`, which will check for the conditions we just discussed. Add the following to `App.vue`:

```
computed: {
  formIsValid() {
    return (
      this.form.firstName.length > 0 &&
      this.form.lastName.length > 0 &&
      this.form.email.length > 0
    );
  }
}
```

Now that we have a computed property checking the state of our form, let's actually use it on the `onSubmit` method. We will verify that `this.formIsValid` is `true`, and if it isn't we will simply return and prevent the form from being submitted. For now, we will only use `console.log` for a confirmation.

Adjust the `onSubmit` method to the following:

```
onSubmit() {
  if (!this.formIsValid) return;
  console.log('Send my form!');
}
```

Go ahead and test this on your browser. If you are missing any fields, you will not get `console.log` as the validation will fail. If you fill them up and hit the **Submit** button, you will get the message in your console.

In the next block, we will incorporate a third-party library, Axios, to help us to send the data.

Bringing in Axios

The next step in our form is to actually have the form send the user's data to our servers. For the sake of example, the data is not going to be actually stored anywhere, but we will look at the steps of creating the POST call that most forms will use for transferring the data to an API or server endpoint.

Axios is a fantastic and popular library for sending and receiving data from servers. I personally recommend it as a go-to whenever you need to make any HTTP calls from your Vue apps. You can find the official GitHub page here: `github.com/axios/axios`.

Follow the next set of steps to get Axios ready on your project:

1. Fire up your Terminal and run the following command:

   ```
   > npm install axios
   ```

2. We are going to need an API endpoint to make our calls to. Since we don't have any servers at hand—and to keep things really simple—we are going to use an app called Mockoon. Head over to mockoon.com/#download and download the app for your OS. Once you have it installed, launch it.

3. In the second column, you are going to see two example routes; the one that we are interested in is the **POST** route to **/dolphins** (frankly, I'm more of a sea otter kind of girl, but I'm rolling with the punches). Go ahead and click the green play triangle on the very top; this will start a server on localhost:3000 as default, but you can change the port if the default doesn't work for you for whatever reason.

4. Now that Axios has been added as a dependency to the project, we can import it into App.vue to make use of its different methods.

5. Add the import statement to the top of the App.vue file, right after the opening <script> tag, and before the export default { line:

   ```
   import axios from 'axios';
   ```

   Thanks to this import, we now have Axios available anywhere in this component. Please keep in mind that if, later on, we want to use it on another component or file, we will have to import it again.

6. Let's update the onSubmit button once more. This time, we will get rid of console.log and then make an async call with Axios:

   ```
   onSubmit() {
     if (!this.formIsValid) return;
     axios
       .post('http://localhost:3000/dolphins', { params: this.form })
       .then(response => {
         console.log('Form has been posted', response);
       }).catch(err => {
         console.log('An error occurred', err);
       });
   }
   ```

A Form in its Simplest Form

Every Axios method returns a promise, which is a vanilla JavaScript object. The `then` block is called whenever this promise resolves, in other words, when the actual HTTP request is completed! For more information about promises, MDN has a great resource at `developer.mozilla.org/en-US/docs/Web/JavaScript/Reference/Global_Objects/Promise`.

If you go to your browser now and try it out, you will see that, when the **Submit** button is clicked, our `onSubmit` method is triggered and `console.log` is successfully executed. At this point, we can say we have a very basic (but sadly useless) form!

Let's take it a little bit further and actually disable the input button until the form is valid. (Remember that our validation is very weak right now, but we will work on it later on.)

Go back to your template, and let's hook up the `:disabled` attribute of the button to our computed property, `formIsValid`:

```
<button
  :disabled="!formIsValid"
  @click.prevent="onSubmit"
  type="submit"
  class="btn btn-primary"
>
  Submit
</button>
```

Once again, test this out in your browser and you will see that the input button is grayed out until the form is actually filled out. Neat!

Summary

In this chapter, we have taken the first steps to create a simple data-gathering form. We styled it using Bootstrap and we hooked into the `<form>` events. Finally, we used Axios and Mockoon to send the data to a dummy backend for testing.

In the next chapter, we will take a look into building reusable form components harnessing the power of Vue.

3
Creating Reusable Form Components

One of the most powerful parts of Vue is its capability to make components.

Components are reusable bits of code that usually include a template, scripts, and styles. The amazing thing about components is that you can box up all the logic for a specific element, or group of elements, into a single unit.

A good way to start thinking in terms of components is to start breaking down everyday objects into simple, smaller pieces. (In your mind please!)

Take, for example, the computer that you are working on. As a whole, the whole system could be called a computer. Now break it down even more—it has a monitor, a keyboard, and cables. Now take the keyboard and break it down. You now have a container, and this container has keys. Each key is a single component, which repeats itself, with some properties that vary between each other. The label on the key changes, and sometimes also the size.

What about this key component? Can you break it down further? Maybe! But is it worth it? A keyboard key is a good single component. It has clear properties that define it, and we could clearly define its internal functionality. When it is pressed, we need to tell whoever is containing it that a key was pressed, and the value of that key.

This process of mentally breaking something down can also be applied to any Vue application. Start out with the app as a whole single unit and break it down.

Right now, our current form is one big blob on `App.vue`, which is less than ideal. Let's create some components!

In this chapter, we will cover the following topics:

- Breaking down an application into reusable components
- Understanding `v-model` in custom components
- Implementing custom input and select components

Technical requirements

The code for this chapter can be found in the following GitHub repository:

https://github.com/PacktPublishing/Building-Forms-with-Vue.js/tree/master/Chapter03.

Check out the following video to see the code in action:

http://bit.ly/2qgj7wx

Breaking down the form into components

Taking a look at `App.vue`, let's start with the smallest possible component that we can create. If you look carefully, you will see a repeating pattern in the code—this is usually a good sign that something could make for a good component!

Within our `<form>` element, we have three different text inputs. Two of them are of `type text`, and one of them is of `type email`. Looks like we will need some way to assign these values to the `type` attribute. A prop object could be a simple solution!

As a quick reminder, here's the current code for the form:

```
<div class="form-group">
  <label>First Name:</label>
  <input v-model="form.firstName" type="text" class="form-control">
</div>
<div class="form-group">
  <label>Last Name:</label>
  <input v-model="form.lastName" type="text" class="form-control">
</div>
<div class="form-group">
  <label>Email:</label>
  <input v-model="form.email" type="email" class="form-control">
</div>
```

Go ahead and create a new file inside the `src/components` folder, naming it `BaseInput.vue`. Personally, I like to name my very basic input components starting with `Base`; that way, I know that it is the simplest possible form of an input that I can find in my application.

If I ever need to make a component that extends or uses `Base` in some way, then I can simply import the `BaseInput` component, and make some adjustments! Do feel free, however, to use any naming convention that you prefer. If you want some actual style guidelines and best practices for naming components and such, refer to the official guide here: https://vuejs.org/v2/style-guide/.

Let's copy over the first input from `App.vue` into our new component inside the `<template>` tags, so that we have a base to work on:

```
<template>
  <div class="form-group">
    <label>Name:</label>
    <input v-model="form.firstName" type="text" class="form-control">
  </div>
</template>
<script>
export default {
}
</script>
```

The first thing we need to do is figure out how to get rid of the hardcoded values; the purpose of extracting code into components is, after all, for them to be dynamic and reusable.

Creating Reusable Form Components

Let's create a prop object to hold the value of `label` (with the name `string`):

```
<script>
export default {
  props: {
    label: {
      type: String,
      required: true
    }
  }
}
</script>
```

We are going to use the extended way to declare properties, with object notation. This way, we can ensure that anyone using our component will at least get yelled at by the console in the browser if they forget to define the label.

Now, let's go back to the template and actually replace this value with the newly created prop object:

```
<template>
  <div class="form-group">
    <label>{{ label }}</label>
    <input v-model="form.firstName" type="text" class="form-control">
  </div>
</template>
```

One more to go, what about the type? We may want to use this (and we will) for email, and eventually password fields.

Let's create a new prop object for this, and bind it, like before:

```
props: {
  label: {
    type: String,
    required: true
  },
  type: {
    type: String,
    default: 'text',
    validator(value) {
      return ['text', 'email', 'password'].includes(value);
    }
  }
}
```

Our new type of property has a default value, which will be used in the event that the prop is missing from the component when it's implemented.

`validator` is a function that, well—validates! It takes a single argument, the value that is getting passed into the property, and it has to return a Boolean to verify that the value is acceptable for the property (`validator` validates!).

In this particular case, we're just checking that it is one of the three choices that we will allow for this component: `text`, `email`, or `password`.

Now that we are set, let's update `<input>`:

```
<input v-model="form.firstName" :type="type" class="form-control">
```

So far, so good! Except that there is one thing still missing, which we have to refactor. Can you spot it?

So far, we have seen how to break down the form into components. Let's now take a deeper look at `v-model`, and its importance when creating dynamic components.

Understanding v-model in custom components

As you know, `v-model` is shorthand for `v-on:input` and `v-bind:value="value"` on a given element. It allows us to two-way bind a particular element's value, and the events that it emits to one of our internal state properties.

When talking about component composition, however, we need to take extra things into consideration.

In order for a custom component to be able to implement the `v-model` contract, we have to make sure that two things happen. That's right! We need to ensure that the component has a `value` property and that it `$emits` an input event.

There is a way to change this default behavior by using the `model` property, but it is out of the scope of this book. If you want to tell your component to use a different property, or a different event for `v-model`, take a look at https://vuejs.org/v2/api/#model.

Creating Reusable Form Components

Let's put this theory into practice. We're going to modify our `BaseInput` component, in order to be able to use a `v-model` binding. First, let's add a `value` property, and hook it to `<input>`:

```
props: {
  label: {
    type: String,
    required: true
  },
  type: {
    type: String,
    default: 'text',
    validator(value) {
      return ['text', 'email', 'password'].includes(value);
    }
  },

  // Add this new prop
  value: {
    type: String,
    required: true
  }
}
```

Now that we have our new `value` prop, we need to bind it to the value of `<input>`. Be sure to remove the old `v-model` from it, though! Have a look at the following example:

```
<input :value="value" type="text" class="form-control">
```

Almost there; now we need to make sure that `<input>` dispatches input events whenever it updates. So, we need to add an event handler that `$emits` this information.

> **Important!** Before we continue, let me tell you about a very common *gotcha* when working with `v-model` and forms. Not all inputs are created equally! The `<input>` text elements (`text`, `email`, and `password`) and `<textarea>` are easy. They fire input events that we can listen to for our `v-model` binding. But, what about `select`, `checkboxes`, and `radio`?

[30]

The Vue documentation makes it super clear, so I'm going to quote it:

> "`v-model` *internally uses different properties and emits different events for different input elements:*
> - `text` *and* `textarea` *elements use* `value` *property and* `input` *event;*
> - `checkboxes` *and* `radiobuttons` *use* `checked` *property and* `change` *event;*
> - `select` *fields use* `value` *as a prop and* `change` *as an event.*"

Now that we have got that theory out of the way, let's actually listen to our event:

```
<input
  :value="value"
  :type="type"
  class="form-control"
  @input="$emit('input', $event.target.value)"
>
```

Congratulations! Our `BaseInput` component is ready to be used.

Now that we have a clear understanding of `v-model` and custom components, we're going to get to use our component inside our form. It will make it far more readable, dynamic, and easy to maintain.

Implementing a custom input component

Creating reusable custom components is a core part of Vue, but for the components to actually be useful, we have to actually *use* them!

Open up your `App.vue` file, and let's replace the three `<div class="form-group">` elements with our custom component.

First things first: what we have to do is import the component to our file. Let's get that out of the way. Add the following import to the top of the `<script>` element, shown as follows:

```
import BaseInput from '@/components/BaseInput';
```

Creating Reusable Form Components

Just importing the file is not enough; we actually have to add the component to the component's property on the file, so that we can then use it inside our template. We currently do not have such a property inside our Vue instance, so let's create one between `name` and `data()`:

```
...
components: { BaseInput },
...
```

Now that we have our component registered, and imported on our `App.vue` file, we can go into the template and replace the old inputs with our new component:

```
<BaseInput
  label="First Name:"
  v-model="form.firstName"
/>
<BaseInput
  label="Last Name:"
  v-model="form.lastName"
/>
<BaseInput
  label="Email:"
  v-model="form.email"
  type="email"
/>
```

Go back to your browser, and play around with the app. You should see that, even though nothing has actually changed, the form is now driven by reusable input components—if we were ever faced with the need to update the inputs' CSS, for example, we could simply change it once in that file, and the whole application would update to reflect those changes.

Open up your Vue DevTools once again, and make sure that you have the first icon selected (the one for the component structure). Drill down into the structure and you will see your three `BaseInput` components represented there.

You can even go ahead and click each one of them, and the **props** panel will clearly display what makes each one of them unique—the props!

Chapter 3

In the following screenshot, you can see that, when I type my name into the **Name:** field, the **<BaseInput>** component reflects it in its **value** property:

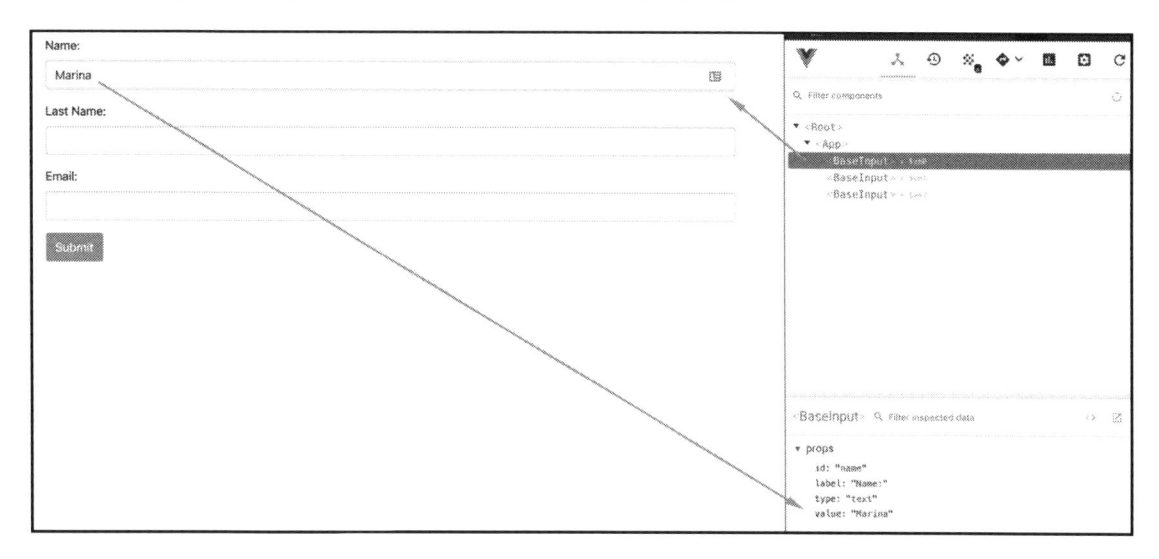

One more thing! Type some values into the form and look at the **props** box, it will update live with the two-way binding in your **value** property. Now, click on the third icon on your DevTools, the one that looks like a bunch of dots—this is the events view.

Type in one of the inputs again, and you will see that the **events** box will fill up with entries. Click on one of them, and you'll notice that our input event is being fired with each keystroke.

These are two different *actions*—the value getting updated and the input event being fired make up for the `v-model` doing its job, as we discussed earlier!

Let's take a look at the following screenshot:

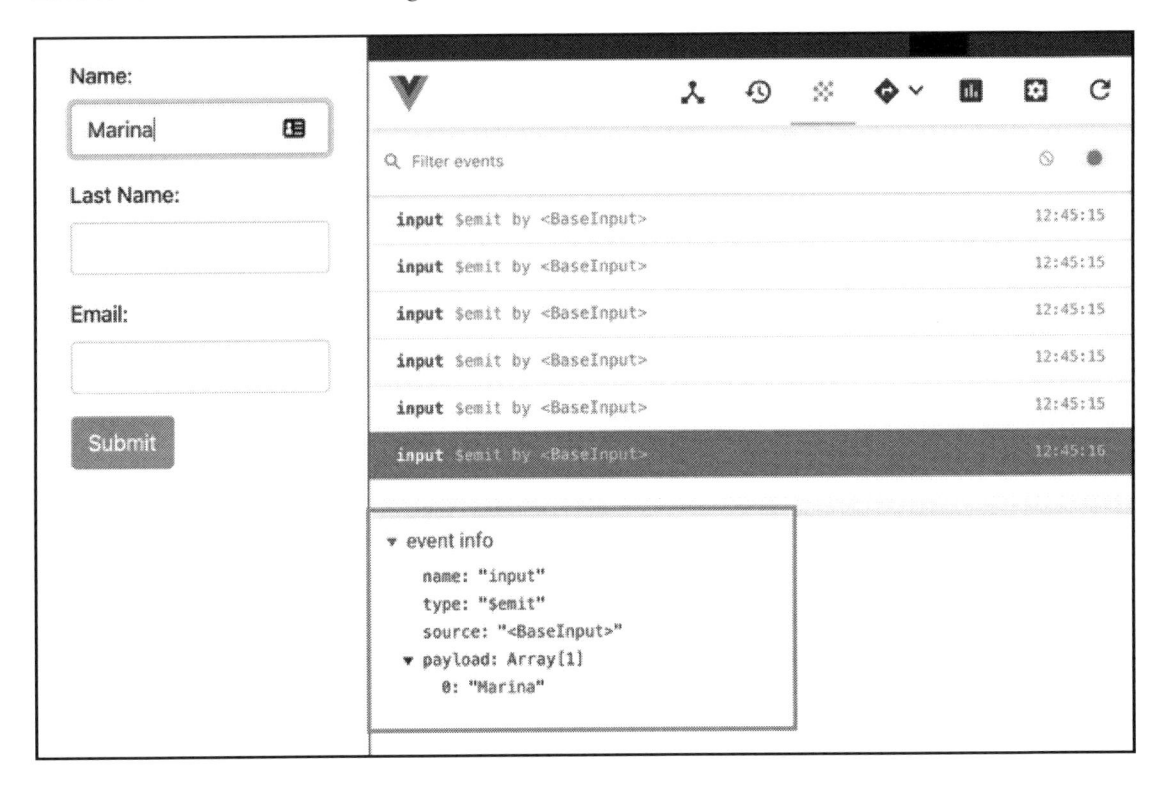

[Screenshot showing a form with Name field containing "Marina", Last Name, Email fields, a Submit button, and Vue DevTools panel displaying input $emit by <BaseInput> events with event info: name: "input", type: "$emit", source: "<BaseInput>", payload: Array[1], 0: "Marina"]

In the preceding screenshot, you can see how the `<BaseInput>` component is emitting input events—`payload` is what the user has typed into the form.

One more time – with dropdowns!

Before we wrap up the chapter, let's build a custom component that wraps up a drop-down input, in order to review what we have learned so far.

Begin by creating the component file—we are going to name it `BaseSelect.vue`, and place it inside the `components` folder.

Just as we did with `BaseInput`, first we are going to define our HTML template. We will leave some attributes empty for now, since we will bind them later. We will also set up some dummy data for easy testing. In component creation, you will find that small steps are the way to go!

Add the following code as a template for `BaseSelect`:

```
<template>
  <div class="form-group">
  <label>Label here</label>
  <select class="form-control">
  <option value="">Test!</option>
  <option value="">Me!</option>
  <option value="">:D</option>
  </select>
  </div>
</template>
```

Looking good! Let's import this new component into `App.vue`, and into our template, so that we can test it in action in our browser. Follow the given steps to do so:

1. Import the component on the top of your `script` element, next to the `BaseInput` import statement:

   ```
   import BaseSelect from '@/components/BaseSelect';
   ```

2. Add `BaseSelect` to your `components` declaration:

   ```
   components: { BaseInput, BaseSelect },
   ```

3. Create an instance of `BaseSelect` inside the `<template>` element, right below the last `BaseInput` component, and before the `div` that holds the input button:

   ```
   ...
   <BaseSelect />
   ...
   ```

Check your browser, and you will see our newly selected component in action. Isn't she beautiful?

Let's take it a step further, we are in dire need of some `props`. Let's start by adding `label`; we can see from the template that it will need to be made dynamic.

Create your `props` object inside a new `script` element, and add it to the list:

```
<script>
export default {
  props: {
    label: {
      type: String,
      required: true
    }
  }
}
</script>
```

Now, head to the template and dynamically bind them. We need to make the contents of `<label>` dynamic with some interpolation:

```
<template>
  <div class="form-group">
    <label>{{ label }}</label>
    <select class="form-control">
      <option value="">Test!</option>
      <option value="">Me!</option>
      <option value="">:D</option>
    </select>
  </div>
</template>
```

So far, so good! Go back to `App.vue`, and add these new `props` to our example component:

```
<BaseSelect
  label="What do you love most about Vue?"
/>
```

Test it out in your browser to make sure nothing is broken. The component is working pretty well so far, but the options it displays are still hardcoded. Let's implement an `options` property—this time it will be an array of objects, which we will use to populate the `select` options.

Go back to `BaseSelect.vue` and create the new property:

```
options: {
  type: Array,
  required: true,
  validator(opts) {
    return !opts.find(opt => typeof opt !== 'object');
  }
}
```

For the `validator` object, we will use the JavaScript array, in order to find a method to see if we can find an element inside the array that is not an object. If something is found, the `find` method will return it and `!` will evaluate it to `false`, which will throw a console error. If nothing is found (and all the elements are objects), then `find` will return `undefined`, which `!` will turn to `true`, and the validation will pass.

For more information about the `find` method, check out the following link: `https://developer.mozilla.org/en-US/docs/Web/JavaScript/Reference/Global_Objects/Array/find`.

Let's go ahead and implement a `v-for` loop inside our `<select>` element:

```
<select class="form-control">
  <option
    v-for="opt in options"
    :key="opt.value"
    :value="opt.value"
  >
    {{ opt.label || 'No label' }}
  </option>
</select>
```

The `v-for` loop will grab each element inside of options, and create a new `<option>` element inside `<select>`; don't forget to set the `:key` property!

If you would like to read more about `:key`, that is, when to use it and why, check out my article at the following link: `https://www.telerik.com/blogs/in-vue-when-do-i-actually-need-the-key-attribute-and-why`.

We will need each object inside options to have a `label` and `value` properties, but we will provide a default in case the `label` is missing.

Go back to `App.vue` and we will create a new internal `state` property inside `data()` called `loveOptions`, which will hold our options for this particular `<Select>`:

```
return {
  form: ...,
  loveOptions: [
    { label: 'Fun to use', value: 'fun' },
    { label: 'Friendly learning curve', value: 'curve' },
    { label: 'Amazing documentation', value: 'docs' },
    { label: 'Fantastic community', value: 'community' }
  ]
}
```

Creating Reusable Form Components

Now that we have set that up, go to the template and bind it to the `options` prop of our `BaseSelect` component:

```
<BaseSelect
  label="What do you love most about Vue?"
  :options="loveOptions"
/>
```

Go back to your browser after you save and check out the options. It's alive!

There is one more thing missing, which we need to add to this component, the `v-model` capabilities. We need to create a `value` prop, make the `option` attribute that is selected use it, and make sure that we fire input events from inside our component.

> *"Remember, remember, the rules of* `v-model`*, the properties bindings and emit. I know of no reason, the* `v-model` *system, should ever be forgot."* - Vue Fawkes

In this case, since we are going to use `v-model` with a `select`, remember that we need to listen to the change, even internally! Another thing to note is that you may be tempted to place a `:value` binding on top of the `select` tag, this is not the correct way of working with selects!

The `<select>` element in HTML does not have a `value` attribute; what it does is apply the `selected` attribute to the `option` element inside of it, which holds the current value:

1. Add the `value` property:

   ```
   value: {
     type: String,
     required: true
   }
   ```

2. You will use the `value` prop to check whether the value of this option is equal to it. Make sure that we emit `input` when the `select` element fires a `change` event:

   ```
   <select
     class="form-control"
     @change="$emit('input', $event.target.value)"
   >
     <option
       v-for="opt in options"
       :key="opt.value"
       :value="opt.value"
       :selected="value === opt.value"
     >
       {{ opt.label || 'No label' }}
   ```

[38]

```
        </option>
      </select>
```

3. Go back to `App.vue` and add the `v-model` binding to this new element. You will need to create a new property called `love` inside the `form` prop in `data()`, and add the `v-model` attribute to the `BaseSelect` element:

   ```
   form: {
     firstName: '',
     lastName: '',
     email: '',
     love: 'fun'
   },
   ```

The `BaseSelect` element will now have a `v-model` binding:

```
<BaseSelect
  label="What do you love most about Vue?"
  :options="loveOptions"
  v-model="form.love"
/>
```

Finally, check in your browser to see that everything is working. Go into DevTools and check your **App** component—you will see that when you switch the value of the select, it too will update!

Summary

In this chapter, we have gone through the process of destructuring a singleton application, or form, into reusable dynamic components. We have covered important core Vue features such as `v-model`, properties, and events.

In the next chapter, we are going to kick it up a notch and implement a very near **user experience** (**UX**) related feature, input masks!

4
Input Masks with v-mask

One of the key aspects of any successful form is clarity. If the user finds the form easy to use and easy to understand, they are more likely to fill it in and submit it. In this chapter, we are going to be looking at input masking. You will learn how to quickly and easily apply masks to your form inputs, and to configure them to your needs with real-life examples, such as telephone numbers.

What exactly are input masks? They are pre-defined structures that display the data for an input. For example, if you were going to mask a telephone input, you'd probably want it to display as **(123) 234-5555**, instead of simply, **1232345555**. You can clearly see that the first example is not only easier to read but it also conveys meaning about what the field is trying to accomplish.

Input masks are a nice feature to take your UX to another level, and they are very easy to implement, thanks to open source libraries such as `v-mask`. The GitHub repository page can be found at the following link: `https://github.com/probil/v-mask`.

In this chapter, we will take a quick look at implementing this library on top of our existing project.

In this chapter, we will cover the following topics:

- Installing the `v-mask` library
- Exploring the `v-mask` directive
- Enhancing our custom inputs

Technical requirements

The code for this chapter can be found in the following GitHub repository:

```
https://github.com/PacktPublishing/Building-Forms-with-Vue.js/tree/master/Chapter04
```

Input Masks with v-mask

Check out the following video to see the code in action:

```
http://bit.ly/31jFmyH
```

Installing the v-mask library

Let's get started with the installation of the `v-mask` library. In order for our project to use what it has to offer, we first need to add it to our project dependencies. Follow these steps in order to do this:

1. Open up your Terminal and type in the following command to add the library to our dependencies:

   ```
   > npm install v-mask
   ```

2. We need to add it to Vue as a plugin, so head to `main.js`, and let's both import it and let Vue know that we want to register it as a plugin for all of our apps. Add the following code, after the `import App` line:

   ```
   import VueMask from 'v-mask'
   Vue.use(VueMask);
   ```

   Now that we have registered our plugin, we have access to a new directive: `v-mask`. We can add this new directive directly onto our `<input>` elements, and the library will handle the masking behind the scenes by reading the user's input, and adjusting the display of the field.

   Let's try this on a regular input first, then we will add some props to our project's component:

3. Go to `App.vue`, and create a new `<input>` element after the email input:

   ```
   <input type="text" />
   ```

   If we were to type a phone number in this field as it is, we would get the default input behavior. Anything goes. So, let's apply a `telephone` number mask to it. Our new `v-mask` library has a requirement that every field that we apply it to needs to be v-modeled, so let's get that done first.

4. Add a new `telephone` prop to our `data()` inside of the `form` object:

   ```
   form: {
     ...
    telephone: ''
   },
   ```

5. Now, go back to our new `<input>` element and apply `v-model`. We are also going to now add the `v-mask` directive, shown as follows:

   ```
   <input
     type="text"
     v-model="form.telephone"
     v-mask="'(###) ###-####'"
   >
   ```

Go back to your browser and try the input once again. As you type, you will see that you are actually getting it nicely formatted to what we would expect for a telephone number.

In five simple steps, we have added input masking to one of our form fields. In the next section, we will go into more depth about what the `v-mask` directive does for us.

Exploring the v-mask directive

When we added the `v-mask` library to our project, and added the plugin within `main.js`, the library created a new directive for us, `v-mask`. What exactly is a directive, though? We know it looks like an HTML attribute, but what else?

A directive can be defined as follows:

> "Directives are special attributes with the v- prefix. Directive attribute values are expected to be a single JavaScript expression (with the exception of `v-for` [...]). A directive's job is to reactively apply side effects to the DOM, when the value of its expression changes". - Official Vue documentation.

Okay, so it looks like we have a special attribute that can modify the element. That sounds exactly like what we saw happen when we applied to the input element. But, how does the actual expression or value that we are putting into this directive work?

We know from the example that we are passing in a string, and you can see that inside the double quotes that make up the `v-mask=""` attribute, we are setting a new pair of single quotes (`'`). This means that the expression inside this attribute is JavaScript, and that we are passing it a string value.

Input Masks with v-mask

From looking at the `v-mask` library documentation, we know that we have a few *special* placeholder characters that we can use inside our masks. The table for those is as follows:

#	Number (0-9)
A	Letter in any case (a-z, A-Z)
N	Number or letter
X	Any symbol
?	Optional (next character)

Take for example a mask that will display the time of the day; you could define it as follows:

```
v-mask="'##:##'"
```

This means that this input will take two numbers, from 0 to 9 (##), followed by a : character, followed by another two numbers (##).

Anything that does not match this pattern will be ignored by the input.

`v-mask` is a very powerful library that allows us to customize exactly how we want our input to be displayed, by combining these simple rules. In the next section, we are going to modify our custom inputs, in order to be able to leverage the power of the input masks.

Enhancing our custom inputs

We have put in a lot of work to create our awesome custom `BaseInput`, so we definitely want to keep using it!

Follow these steps in order to modify `BaseInput` and to allow for input masking:

1. Go back to `App.vue` and switch the `<input>` element for a `<BaseInput>` component:

    ```
    <BaseInput
    label="Telephone"
     type="text"
     v-model="form.telephone"
    />
    ```

Let's go into `BaseInput.vue` now and create a new prop; we will call it `mask`, and it will default to an empty string. It is important that we default it to an empty string, or else the directive will try to match it, and we won't be able to type into the fields if they don't have a declared mask!

2. Add it to your `props` object:

   ```
   ...,
   mask: {
   type: String,
   required: false
   }
   ```

3. Now, go back to `App.vue` and update our telephone `BaseInput` to use the `mask` attribute:

   ```
   <BaseInput
   label="Telephone"
   type="text"
   v-model="form.telephone"
     :mask="'(###) ###-####'"
   />
   ```

All done! Return to your browser, and add some numbers in the field and you should have a nice-looking telephone mask working with your custom component!

Summary

In this chapter, we have learned how to leverage the power of the `v-mask` library in order to apply input masking to our forms. Input masking is a powerful, yet easy way to grant our users a better experience, and it should not be overlooked when building even the simplest forms!

In the next chapter, we are going to take it up a notch and look at form validation with a powerful library: `Vuelidate`!

5
Input Validation with Vuelidate

In production-ready forms, validating user input is a must. Even though, on the server side, applications should double-check all the data that is passed to them, also pre-validating data on the frontend should be a mandatory practice for any experienced developer.

In this chapter, we are going to look at a very well-known and powerful library for form validation, Vuelidate. You will learn how to use this library in your projects, and you will be able to successfully validate user input with it.

Thankfully, in Vue, we have a few different options for third-party libraries, such as Vuelidate, VeeValidate, and even Vuetify has its own validation methods.

In this chapter, we will be covering Vuelidate. Ranging from its installation to the creation of rules and applying them to our form inputs, and using the error state to inform our users of a problem.

This chapter will cover the following topics:

- Installing dependencies
- Creating validation rules
- Moving validation into our custom inputs
- Adding the final touches

Technical requirements

The code for this chapter can be found in the following GitHub repository:

```
https://github.com/PacktPublishing/Building-Forms-with-Vue.js/tree/master/Chapter05.
```

Check out the following video to see the code in action:

```
http://bit.ly/2VJIL8E
```

Installing dependencies

Let's start by installing Vuelidate in our project as a dependency, and then we are going to use it for validation. Follow these steps:

1. Open up the Terminal and execute the following command:

   ```
   > npm install vuelidate
   ```

   Once the library has been installed, we have to import it into `main.js` and use it as a plugin, so that it is globally available to all our components.

2. Add the following code to `main.js`, after the code that imports `Vue` and `App`:

   ```
   import Vuelidate from 'vuelidate';
   Vue.use(Vuelidate);
   ```

Now that Vuelidate has been installed and is now part of our project dependencies, we are ready to make it do some of the heavy lifting. In the next section, we are going to create our validation rules.

Creating validation rules

When we added Vuelidate to our project through `Vue.use`, the library added a new reserved property that we can use on our components: `validations`.

This property is added onto the configuration object for the component, alongside `data()`, `computed`, and so on. It will also be an object that holds a property of its own for each input that we want to validate.

Let's create this property and set up a new input, without a custom component wrapper to test. Once we understand the basics, we can work on translating all of this into our `BaseInput` and `BaseSelect` components.

Follow these steps in order to create validation rules:

1. Create a new `<input>` form below the `telephone` object of `BaseInput` in `App.vue`:

   ```
   <input type="text" v-model="form.website" />
   ```

2. Remember to add this new property, `website`, to the `form` object of `data()`:

   ```
   form: {
     firstName: '',
     lastName: '',
     email: '',
     love: 'fun',
     telephone: '',
     website: ''
   },
   ```

   Now, let's go and actually create a `validations` property; for now, we will only add the `form.website` validations.

3. Place it on the top level of the `component` object, at the same level as your `data()` and computed properties:

   ```
   validations: {
     form: {
       website: {
         // our validations will go here
       }
     }
   }
   ```

   For this particular field, we want to make sure that we validate that the input that the user provides, is a valid URL. In Vuelidate, we have several different built-in validators that we can use out of the box. A complete list can be found at `https://vuelidate.netlify.com/#sub-builtin-validators`.

   In order to validate that the input is a valid URL, we have the URL validator. But, in order for us to add it to our website's `validators` object, we have to import it first. Vuelidate allows us to import only the validators that we are actually going to be using; that way, we can ensure that our deployed code stays smaller.

4. Add the following import statement to `App.vue`, near the other imports:

   ```
   import { url } from 'vuelidate/lib/validators';
   ```

Input Validation with Vuelidate

5. Now that we have imported the statement, we can finally add it to the `validations.website` object:

    ```
    validations: {
      form: {
        website: {
           url // Validate that the "website" input is a valid URL
        }
      }
    },
    ```

    That's enough of setting up our rules. Remember the new `<input>` form that we created earlier to hold `v-model="form.website"`? We're going to need to make some adjustments to the way that `v-model` is set up, in order for Vuelidate to take charge of the validation.

    Apart from the `validations` property that we used earlier to set up our rules, Vuelidate gives us access to a new property inside the component instance: `$v`.

    `$v` is a special object that holds a copy of our validation structure. Among other things, a notable trait is that it has a `$model` property for each one of the elements that we added to `validations`. Vuelidate will become an *intermediary* model for us, and in turn, it will take care of actually binding to our `form.website` property within `data()`, automatically.

    Let's look at this in practice:

6. Update the `<input>` website element to use the new `v-model` format that Vuelidate expects. Also, we are going to interpolate the `$v` object below it, so that you can see more clearly what's happening behind the scenes, as follows:

    ```
    <input type="text" v-model="$v.form.website.$model" />
    <pre>{{ $v }}</pre>
    ```

7. Go back to your browser and take a look at the structure of the `$v` object, before you type anything in your new form field.

    The first thing to pay special attention to is the `form.website` object. Inside this object, Vuelidate will keep the validation state of this input. The `$model` property will hold the user's input, just as we told `v-model` to do. The `$error` property is the one that will actually toggle a Boolean value, and will let us know if there was an error in the input.

Try typing some random gibberish in the field and observe the properties that get updated. The $error property will update to true, to indicate that there is an error. The url property, which is directly tied to the URL rule, will switch to false, to indicate that the URL validation condition is not being met.

8. Let's add some CSS binding onto <input>, in order to visually display that something is not passing validation on our input:

```
<input
  type="text"
  v-model="$v.form.website.$model"
  class="form-control"
  :class="{
    'is-valid': !$v.form.website.$error && $v.form.website.$dirty,
    'is-invalid': $v.form.website.$error
  }"
/>
```

Try this in your browser before we go into a further explanation. Try typing a valid URL, such as http://google.com, and notice how the input changes to reflect your changes.

The :class binding is a way to add classes conditionally to any HTML element in Vue. In the type of syntax that we are using here, an object, it allows us to set up a key-value pair, in which the key defines the class that we want to be toggled, for example, is-valid.

The value is a JavaScript condition that will be evaluated, in order to determine whether or not the class should be applied. These conditions are reactive, and will be re-executed every time the dependencies of the condition change.

In our example, is-valid will be toggled *on*, whenever there is no $error and the input is $dirty. If you're wondering why we have to check against $dirty as well, try removing that part of the condition and then reload your browser. You'll notice right away that the green border and checkmark are present on the input, even if the element doesn't have any value in it. The way we determine whether <input> has been modified by the user at any point is through the $dirty property; in this case, it makes sense from a UX perspective to not show the valid visual queues until there's actually some input there.

In the case of is-invalid, we are checking to see if there are any $errors present in the field, and setting the field up with a nice red border and an **x** icon.

Now that we have some basic rules in place, let's move on to the next section, where we will learn how to incorporate all of this into our custom components.

Moving validation into our custom inputs

The amazing thing about having your own custom components is that you can craft them in any way you like. For this chapter, we're going to add support for both a valid and an invalid status to our components. The main validation logic will still be held by the parent, `App.vue`, as it is the containing component that holds our form.

Follow these steps to add validations:

1. First, let's add new rules for each of our inputs. Add the following to the `validations` property:

    ```
    validations: {
    form: {
    first_name: { alpha, required },
    last_name: { alpha },
        email: { email, required },
      telephone: {
          validPhone: phone => phone.match(/((\(\d{3}\) ?)|(\d{3}-))?
          \d{3}-\d{4}/) !== null
        },
        website: { url },
        love: { required }
      }
    },
    ```

2. Don't forget to update your import statement to bring in the new validators that we are now using, as follows:

    ```
    import { url, alpha, email, required } from
    'vuelidate/lib/validators';
    ```

    Let's go over the new validators:

    - `alpha`: This will restrict the field to only alpha-numeric characters.
    - `required`: This field makes the field required; it is invalid if there is no value.
    - `email`: This field ensures that the input holds a valid email format.

    For the `telephone` field, we're going to do some custom validation, because this field is masked to have a specific format, `(###) ###-####`, and we need to resort to writing our own validation function.

Chapter 5

In this case, we're calling the validator, `validPhone`, and it is a function that returns a Boolean value. This Boolean is calculated by matching the phone against a regular expression and assuring that it is not null; that is, that it does, in fact, have a match.

Now that we have all our `validations` in place, we have to update our `App.vue` template. Our `BaseInput` components and the `BaseSelect` component need to have `v-model` updated, so that it points to the Vuelidate model instead of our local state. Also, we need to update our website input to a full `BaseInput` component.

3. Make the following changes to your code; we are updating `v-model` and the input types:

```
<form>
  <BaseInput
    label="First Name:"
    v-model="$v.form.firstName.$model"
  />
  <BaseInput
    label="Last Name:"
    v-model="$v.form.lastName.$model"
  />
  <BaseInput
    label="Email:"
    v-model="$v.form.email.$model"
    type="email"
  />
  <BaseInput
    label="The URL of your favorite Vue-made website"
    v-model="$v.form.website.$model"
  />
  <BaseInput
    label="Telephone"
    type="text"
    v-model="$v.form.telephone.$model"
    :mask="'(###) ###-####'"
  />
  <BaseSelect
    label="What do you love most about Vue?"
    :options="loveOptions"
    v-model="$v.form.love.$model"
  />
  <div class="form-group">
    <button
      :disabled="!formIsValid"
```

[53]

Input Validation with Vuelidate

```
      @click.prevent="onSubmit"
      type="submit"
      class="btn btn-primary"
    >Submit</button>
  </div>
</form>
```

In order for our custom components to display the correct CSS classes, we are going to add a new prop to them called `validator`, and we will pass the reference to the Vuelidate object's prop that matches this particular element.

4. Open `BaseInput.vue` and create the `validator` property, as follows:

```
validator: {
type: Object,
  required: false,
  validator($v) {
    return $v.hasOwnProperty('$model');
  }
}
```

In the `validator` method for the property, we are going to check that the `validator` object that got passed in as a property has a `$model` property in it (that is, `validator.$model`), which is `true` for all of the field props of Vuelidate. That way, we can ensure that we have access to the properties that we need.

Next, let's bring over the `:class` binding that we had before on our `<input>` element, but we will make some slight adjustments, to account for this being a `component` property.

5. Add the following to the `<input>` element inside `BaseInput.vue`:

```
:class="{
  'is-valid': validator && !validator.$error && validator.$dirty,
  'is-invalid': validator && validator.$error
}"
```

Since `validator` is not a required prop on our component, we have to double-check that the condition that is actually set before checking its `$error` and `$dirty` properties.

6. Finally, go back to `App.vue` and add the `:validator` attribute to all of our `BasicInput` elements:

```
<BaseInput
  label="First Name:"
  v-model="$v.form.firstName.$model"
  :validator="$v.form.firstName"
/>
<BaseInput
  label="Last Name:"
  v-model="$v.form.lastName.$model"
  :validator="$v.form.lastName"
/>
<BaseInput
  label="Email:"
  v-model="$v.form.email.$model"
  :validator="$v.form.email"
  type="email"
/>
<BaseInput
  label="The URL of your favorite Vue-made website"
  v-model="$v.form.website.$model"
  :validator="$v.form.website"
/>
<BaseInput
  label="Telephone"
  type="text"
  v-model="$v.form.telephone.$model"
  :validator="$v.form.telephone"
  :mask="'(###) ###-####'"
/>
```

Go back to your browser and play around with the inputs, now that they are all being validated behind the scenes by Vuelidate!

Whew, that was quite a bit of information—grab yourself a break and some avocado toast; you deserve it! In the next section, we are going to make some final changes to our form, to `BaseSelect`, and to our `onSubmit` method, so that we can wrap things up.

Adding the final touches

There are a couple more things that we need to do before we can close off this chapter. First of all, let's take care of `BaseSelect`; it still needs a `validator` property and some `:class` bindings.

Follow these steps to find out how we can do this:

1. First, add the `validator` prop in `BaseSelect.vue`:

   ```
   validator: {
   type: Object,
    required: false,
     validator($v) {
       return $v.hasOwnProperty('$model');
     }
   }
   ```

   Now, let's add the `:class` binding; except here, we're not going to check against `$dirty`, because we don't have an initial empty value.

2. Add the following code to the `<select>` element:

   ```
   :class="{
     'is-valid': validator && !validator.$error,
     'is-invalid': validator && validator.$error
   }"
   ```

3. Now that the component is ready, go back to `App.vue` and update our `BaseSelect` element with its own `:validator` attribute:

   ```
   <BaseSelect
     label="What do you love most about Vue?"
     :options="loveOptions"
     v-model="$v.form.love.$model"
     :validator="$v.form.love"
   />
   ```

4. Go back to your browser and verify that the element is behaving as expected.

   Another thing that we shouldn't forget to change is our `onSubmit` method on `App.vue`. Right now, we are using a `computed` property that is doing a very poor job of checking the validity of our form. Let's fix this by leveraging some more of Vuelidate's power to check whether our form is ready to submit. To do this, let's delete our `formIsValid computed` property first.

Vuelidate has an `$invalid` property on the root of the `$v` object, which we can check to see whether the form is ready for submission. We are going to use this in a minute for our `onSubmit` method.

5. Delete the `formIsValid computed` property completely:

   ```
   computed: {}
   ```

   By default, all forms start out as having an `$invalid` state, because Vuelidate triggers its validations when the user `$touches` and modifies the input fields. We need to make some slight adjustments in order to accommodate this behavior with our Submit button.

6. Change the button's `:disabled` attribute first, in order to check against `$error`, instead of our old `computed` property:

   ```
   <button
     :disabled="$v.$error"
     @click.prevent="onSubmit"
     type="submit"
     class="btn btn-primary"
   >Submit</button>
   ```

7. Next, let's modify the `onSubmit` method to both force the `$touch` method of all the inputs (and to trigger the validations on all of them), and to check afterward whether the form is actually valid and ready for submitting:

   ```
   onSubmit() {
     this.$v.$touch();
     if (!this.$v.$invalid) return;
     axios.post('http://localhost:3000/dolphins', { params:
     this.form }).then(response => {
     console.log('Form has been posted', response);
     }).catch(err => {
     console.log('An error occurred', err);
     });
   }
   ```

Go back to your browser and reload the window to clear the inputs. Without typing anything, click on the **Submit** button. You will see that the `$v.$touch()` method will trigger and the invalid inputs (such as those that are required, for example) will turn to red to indicate that there is a problem.

Input Validation with Vuelidate

In the following screenshot, you can see how `validator` is working, and how it is visually confirming to the user, what is happening:

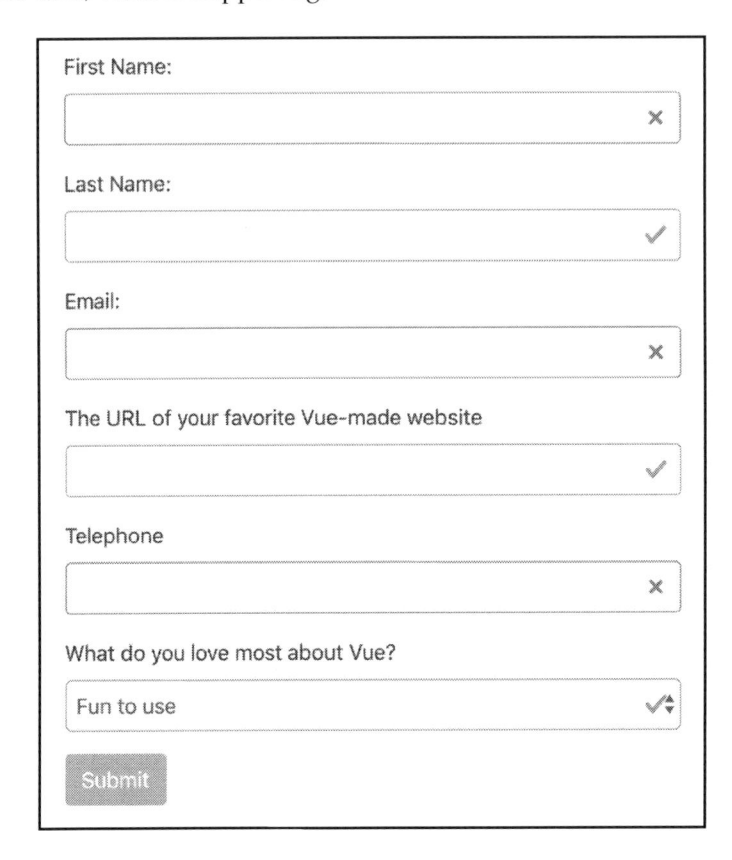

That's it! Vuelidate is a fantastic tool when it comes to form validation—it is super flexible, and allows for hooking into external data sources such as Vuex, which we will see in the next chapter.

Summary

In this chapter, you have learned how to add Vuelidate as a dependency to your Vue project, as well as acquiring the skills to set up and manage form validation on regular inputs and on custom components. In the next chapter, we are going to take things one step further and look at global state management with—*drum roll*—Vuex!

6
Moving to a Global State with Vuex

Vuex is a state management pattern and library. Wait, what? Let's put all of the technical lingo aside for this one—if you want to read the official technical explanation, you can do so on the official Vuex website, **What is Vuex?**, at https://vuex.vuejs.org/.

In this chapter, you are going to learn how to set up your project using the global state management pattern and library, Vuex. Vuex will allow you to extract local state from your components into a, well, global all-knowing state. If you're not familiar with this type of pattern, such as React's Redux, don't worry! Keep reading—we're going to take baby steps.

We're going to approach it on a what-does-that-mean-for-me level. As you probably know, the way that components in Vue communicate is through props from the parent to the children and events from the children to the parent. The children components, in some cases, will want to send data back to their parents. Maybe you want to alert the parent that something inside of it was clicked, or some piece of data was changed. In our previous example, our `BasicInput` and `BasicSelect` components `$emit` values to the parent when they change or when an input happens.

In some cases, the parent component has a parent of its own and `$emits` something up to it as well. Sometimes, this third parent has a parent and so on. This can quickly become a very complex web of components that is flawlessly communicating with each other in perfect balance. Or so you thought.

You get a call from your client: they want you to make an API call on your app that displays the name of the current user on the header, and they want you to pre-populate some fields on the form if there is a currently logged-in user. What do you do? Perhaps you're thinking about making the API call on the `App.vue` parent component and start building a chain of props down the components that need it, but what would happen when that data changes on one of the children? Will you `$emit` the value back to the parents and create a massive chain?

The solution is to use Vuex. Vuex will provide you with a global state that is not attached to any of your components directly but is accessible to all of them. In this chapter, we will grab our work from the previous chapter and migrate the whole form to Vuex. We will also make a mock API call to pull a logged-in user's data and pre-populate our global store with some values.

The following topics will be covered in this chapter:

- Adding Vuex to our project
- Creating the mock API endpoint
- Creating the global state
- Adding some mutations
- Lights, Vue, action!
- Vuelidate and Vuex

Technical requirements

The complete code for this chapter can be found in the following GitHub repository:

`https://github.com/PacktPublishing/Building-Forms-with-Vue.js/tree/master/Chapter06`.

Check out the following video to see the code in action:

`http://bit.ly/31l16Kg`

Adding Vuex to our project

Let's start by adding Vuex to our project. Follow these steps:

1. Open up the Terminal and run the following command to get Vuex added to the project as a dependency:

    ```
    > npm install vuex
    ```

2. Now that we have the library installed, we need to add it as a plugin to our app. Go to `main.js`, import it and add it with the following lines of code. You can place them after the `Vue` and `App` import statements:

```
import Vuex from 'vuex';
Vue.use(Vuex);
const store = new Vuex.store({
  // Our global store
});
```

The `store` variable will hold all of our global states, including our actions and mutations as well. We'll discuss those in more detail soon. For `store` to be available to the whole app, we are missing one last step. We need to inject the `store` variable into our `Vue` instance.

3. Inside `main.js` still, go to the configuration options for the new `Vue` instance and inject `store` to it as a property:

```
new Vue({
store: store,
  render: h => h(App),
}).$mount('#app');
```

Great job! Now that we have Vuex set up as a project dependency, we can almost dive into creating our store—there's just one more tiny thing to do before that. We're going to create a quick mock API endpoint for our testing.

Creating the mock API endpoint

To simulate that we are making an HTTP call to an API to get the details of our user, we need to set it up first using Mockoon. If you don't have it set up, check the instructions on how to install it in `Chapter 2`, *A Form in its Simplest Form*, in the *Bringing in Axios* section of this book.

Moving to a Global State with Vuex

Let's look at how to create a mock API endpoint. Follow these steps:

1. Open up the app and click on the **Add route** button in the second column. This will add a new route to the list in that same column. Click on it to select it and the pane on the right-hand side will update to show the information for this particular route:

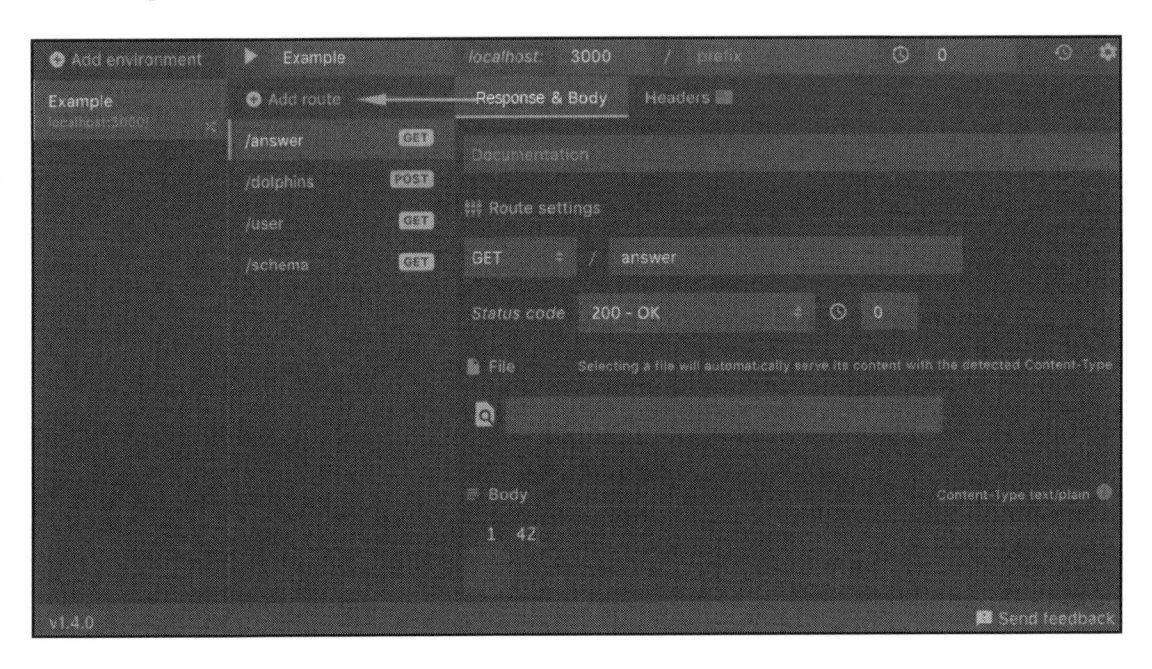

2. Under **Route settings**, where you can input the name of the route, leave the verb as **GET** and set the name of the endpoint as `user`:

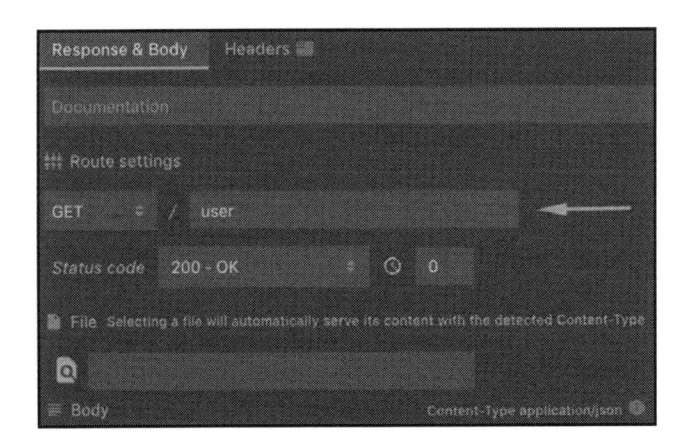

3. Now, go to the **Body** section of the panel and set up the dummy data that we will be returning from our call. Feel free, of course, to fill this with your own name and dummy information shown as follows:

```
{
    "firstName": "Marina",
    "lastName": "Mosti",
    "email": "marina@test.com",
    "love": "fun",
    "telephone": "(800)555-5555",
    "website": "http://dev.to/marinamosti"
}
```

The following screenshot shows how the dummy information will look like:

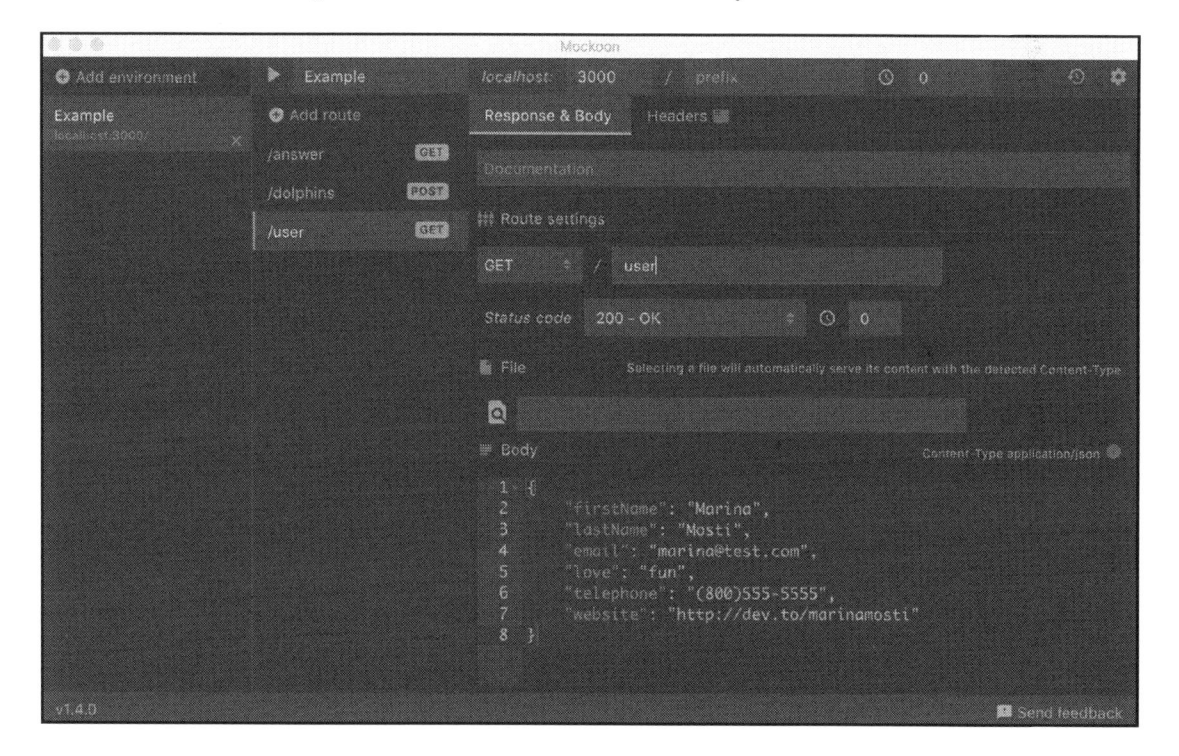

4. One more thing before we start our mock server. Go to the **Headers** tab on the top of the panel, and add a new header. The left side should read **Content-Type** and the right side should read `application/json`, as shown in the following screenshot:

Finally, make sure that you start the server with the green play icon on the toolbar. If the server was already running, click the stop button and restart it.

Mockoon is a super simple but powerful tool, and, with these easy steps, we have a fully functional endpoint to run tests with. In the next section, we are going to finally dive into creating our store and, with it, the global state.

Creating the global state

Now that we are done with the setup, we can go back to `main.js` and start working on our global state.

Inside the new `Vuex.Store` configuration, we will add a reserved property called `state`. `state` is a reactive object that works in a similar way to the local state, `data()`, so we will redefine the structure of our form here, except, since it's not directly tied to it now, we will rename it `user`.

Back in `main.js`, go ahead and set up the following state inside the new `Vuex.Store` object:

```
state: {
  user: {
    firstName: '',
    lastName: '',
    email: '',
    love: 'fun',
    telephone: '',
    website: ''
  }
},
```

You may be wondering why we are naming our global property that holds the user data as `user` instead of `form` as we had it before. First, let me clarify that you are free to name your state variables as best fits the needs of your application! However, in this case, `form` doesn't really clarify at a glance what kind of data we will be storing here; on the other hand, `user` is super descriptive.

A common practice is to have the `user` property here start out as null. In that case, you can check whether they're already authenticated with simple `if` statements such as `if (!user)`. In this case, I have opted for this setup for clarity of the structure. Sure, in `App.vue`, the user's data will be used to populate a form, but in another part of our application, it may be used to display some of the user's data outside any type of form.

Learning how to set up your store is the first step to successfully having a functional global state. In the following section, we are going to add the ability to modify this store with mutations.

Adding some mutations to our store

One important thing to know about Vuex is that, even though the global state is accessible from any of our components, we should not directly mutate or modify it. To modify the content of our user, we will need to create something called **mutations**. Mutations are methods that have one single job: to accept a value or payload and to commit a modification to the state. That way, Vuex can keep tabs on which components are making modifications to the state without it becoming highly chaotic!

Let's create our first mutation; we will call it `updateUser`.

This mutation will take two parameters: the first one is `state`. Every mutation will always receive the state as the first parameter; it is injected to mutations by Vuex by default. The second parameter will be the value that that mutation will get when you call it—in this case, we will call it `user` since that is what we will pass down to it. It is important to know that mutations *cannot* execute asynchronous code. Every mutation needs to be synchronous because they are making changes to our state directly.

Create a new property inside the `Vuex.Store` configuration called `mutations` and then add our following new mutation to it:

```
mutations: {
  updateUser(state, user) {
    state.user = user;
  },
},
```

When this mutation is committed, it will update the global state by calling `state.user = user` with the user that we pass through it. Now, where exactly do we want to commit this new mutation?

Earlier, we set up an API endpoint to fetch our mock *logged-in* user. We still have to set up a call to this endpoint so that our application can use it when it starts to check whether there is a user from the API.

Lights, Vue, actions!

The third key part of Vuex is called **actions**. Actions are methods, just as mutations are, but they can perform asynchronous code within them.

Actions receive two parameters as follows:

- The first one is a `context`, which is an object that holds a reference to the state, the getters, and the ability to commit mutations and dispatch other actions.
- The second (optional) parameter is user-defined; means that we can send extra information to our actions if we need it, but this can also be safely ignored.

A common pattern in Vuex-powered applications is to keep HTTP calls inside Vuex actions—that way, they can be dispatched by any component inside the application if they are needed. These HTTP calls usually modify or make use of the state, which is very convenient since we have this all available through the `context`.

Let's go back to the problem at hand. We need to make a call to our `/users` endpoint to get the user's information. We are going to create a Vuex action called `getLoggedInUser` that will know how to make this call for us and will automatically commit the information it fetches to the state.

Follow these steps:

1. Since we will be using Axios for this, make sure that we first import it to `main.js` at the top of the file with the other import statements:

   ```
   import axios from 'axios';
   ```

2. Now, create a property called `actions` inside the `Vuex.Store` configuration object; this property is also a reserved word. Inside of it, we will create our `getLoggedInUser` function:

   ```
   getLoggedInUser(context) {
       axios.get('http://localhost:3000/user')
       .then(response => {
         context.commit('updateUser', response.data);
       });
   },
   ```

Remember that Axios returns a JavaScript promise, so we will attach a `.then` block to our call in which we will commit our `updateUser` mutation with the data of the response. This data is exactly the one that we defined earlier in Mockoon as a JSON object. Keep in mind that a real-life application would involve a more intricate process for checking whether the user is, in fact, logged-in; a common practice would be to pass in an ID, of sorts, to the endpoint, or perhaps even the backend will handle the session by passing tokens back and forth. However, this is beyond the scope of this book, so we will keep on using this fake scenario for demo purposes.

Moving to a Global State with Vuex

Now that we have our action ready, we need a place to dispatch it. In this case, we are going to assume that our app wants to check for the logged-in user as soon as possible, so we are going to leverage the `created()` hook inside our `App.vue` file:

1. Head to `App.vue` and add the `created` method onto the component:

   ```
   created() {
     this.$store.dispatch('getLoggedInUser');
   }
   ```

2. Open your browser, refresh the page, and check your **Network** tab on the developer tools. You'll see that, as soon as the page is loaded, our Axios call to `http://localhost:3000/user` is being fired, and the user's data is being loaded. If you have an error, remember to start the server on Mockoon first!

3. Before we move onto modifying our form, let's make a new `<TheHeader>` component to showcase the power of our new global state. Create a new file, `TheHeader.vue`, inside the `components` folder and copy the following code:

   ```
   <template>
     <div class="row">
       <div class="col-12 text-right">
         <p v-if="$store.state.user">
           Welcome back, {{ $store.state.user.firstName }}!
         </p>
       </div>
     </div>
   </template>
   ```

   In this component, we're going to use interpolation to output `$store.state.user.firstName`, which, in turn, will access our global state, inside the state, and inside the user and look for the `firstName` property and display it here.

4. Go back to `App.vue` and import the component:

   ```
   import 'TheHeader' from '@/components/TheHeader'
   ```

   Don't forget to declare it inside the `components` property, as follows:

   ```
   components: { BaseInput, BaseSelect, TheHeader },
   ```

5. Finally, add our new component to the template right below the opening `<div>` element and check it out on the browser. You should see the name of our user being output directly from the global state:

```
<div id="app" class="container py-4">
    <TheHeader />
    ...
```

Now that you understand both actions and mutations, we can take the difficulty up a notch. In the next section, we are going to incorporate our two major libraries—Vuex and Vuelidate.

Vuelidate and Vuex

For our form to continue to work with Vuelidate alongside Vuex, we are going to have to make some adjustments to how we have our data set up for two-way binding on our inputs. Don't worry, we'll take it step by step. Now that we have Vuex incorporated into our app, we want our form to use our global state instead of the local state we had in our `data() { form: {...} }` inside `App.vue`. So, we need to make some changes in our template to tell the two-way binding to use Vuex instead.

We are going to remove all of the `v-model` statements from the inputs in our form. Instead, we are going to manually create our two-way bindings by setting up the `:value` bind and the `@input` listener.

First, we will create a new method called `updateUser`, which will receive two parameters, as follows:

- The first one will be `property` in our form that is getting updated, for example, `firstName` or `lastName`.
- The second parameter will be the `value` that this new property will receive.

So, let's start by adding this new method to our `App.vue` component:

```
updateUser(property, value) {
  this.$store.dispatch('updateUserData', {
    property,
    value
  });

  this.$v.form[property].$touch();
}
```

This method will dispatch a new action that we will create in a moment called `updateUserData`; it will send a payload with the `property` and the `value` that the method got.

Let's stop for a minute and look at the second statement. Since Vuelidate will no longer be hooked into our local state, it is going to need us to tell it when to recalculate the dirty state of the input and to check for errors in validation.

Since the `updateUser` method will be in charge of making the changes to our global state, we will access Vuelidate's object for this input through `$v.form[property]` and force `$touch()` on it.

Now that our state will be global, we don't need our `form: {...}` local state anymore, so you can go ahead and delete it. Your `data()` prop should now look like the following:

```
data() {
  return {
    loveOptions: [
      { label: 'Fun to use', value: 'fun' },
      { label: 'Friendly learning curve', value: 'curve' },
      { label: 'Amazing documentation', value: 'docs' },
      { label: 'Fantastic community', value: 'community' }
    ]
  }
},
```

However, for Vuelidate to be able to access our global state, we are going to need to use a Vuex helper function to map it to computed properties. In this case, we want to use `mapState`. Imagine if you had to create a computed property for each one of our user properties, you would have to go down the list and create a lot of duplicated code that looked like the following example:

```
firstName() {
  return this.$store.state.user.firstName;
}
```

Imagine having to do this for all the properties of your form, could get tedious fast, right?

In these cases, Vuex has some handy map functions that we can leverage, so let's go ahead and import `mapState` to the top of our `App.vue` file:

```
import { mapState } from 'vuex';
```

Next, we will add a `computed` prop to our `App.vue` component and use the `mapState` function to map our whole state to the computed properties:

```
computed: {
  ...mapState({form: 'user'}),
},
```

We are going to pass an object to `mapState` to tell the function exactly what part of our whole global state we want to map to our computed properties. In this case, we are telling it to map everything inside the user global state to a local form. Since the user is an object with several child properties, it will create a binding for each one of them, so that when `App.vue` calls, for example, `this.form.firstName`, it will be found in the global state in `this.$store.state.user.firstName`. Awesome, right?!

Keep in mind that `mapState` returns an object, so we can use the JavaScript ES6 spread operator here to merge the newly created into our `computed: {}` prop. This is incredibly handy if you want to add some more computed properties later, which are not mapped from Vuex.

If you want to learn more about the spread operator, please refer to the following article: https://dev.to/marinamosti/understanding-the-spread-operator-in-javascript-485j.

Before we go and work on the `updateUserData` action, let's make the `v-model` change that we discussed to our inputs. Remove all of the `v-model` statements, and replace them on each one as follows:

```
<BaseInput
  label="First Name:"
  :value="$store.state.user.firstName"
  @input="updateUser('firstName', $event)"
  :validator="$v.form.firstName"
/>
<BaseInput
  label="Last Name:"
  :value="$store.state.user.lastName"
  @input="updateUser('lastName', $event)"
  :validator="$v.form.lastName"
/>
<BaseInput
  label="Email:"
  :value="$store.state.user.email"
  @input="updateUser('email', $event)"
  :validator="$v.form.email"
  type="email"
```

Moving to a Global State with Vuex

```
/>
<BaseInput
  label="The URL of your favorite Vue-made website"
  :value="$store.state.user.website"
  @input="updateUser('website', $event)"
  :validator="$v.form.website"
/>
<BaseInput
  label="Telephone"
  type="text"
  :value="$store.state.user.telephone"
  @input="updateUser('telephone', $event)"
  :validator="$v.form.telephone"
  :mask="'(###)###-####'"
/>
<BaseSelect
  label="What do you love most about Vue?"
  :options="loveOptions"
  :value="$store.state.user.love"
  @input="updateUser('love', $event)"
  :validator="$v.form.love"
/>
```

The `:value` property will bind to our global state, that is, the one we created at the beginning of this chapter. The `$store` property is accessible globally through our application thanks to Vuex, and we can use it to access the state directly, even in our templates. The `@input` listeners will point directly to `updateUser`, set the property as a string, and pass the payload of the `$event` as the value.

Head over to `main.js`; we have to create the new action that our `updateUser` method is calling. We are going to leverage our already existing mutation, `updateUser`, to update one of the properties of the user. You could also refactor this into a mutation that specifically just updates one of the properties instead of overwriting the whole object. In this case, the object is very small, and the performance is not a concern. Add the following action to your store:

```
updateUserData(context, payload) {
  const userCopy = {...context.state.user};
  userCopy[payload.property] = payload.value;
  context.commit('updateUser', userCopy);
}
```

On the first line of the action, we are going to make a shallow copy of our user state by using ES6's spread operator. It's important to keep in mind that the state should never be changed outside of a mutation, so if we assign the new property value directly to the user in our state, we would be doing exactly that.

After making the copy, we set the property to the new value and call `commit` on our `updateUser` mutation. Go back to your browser and reload the page; make sure you have the dummy Mockoon API running so that our Axios calls work and check out the results:

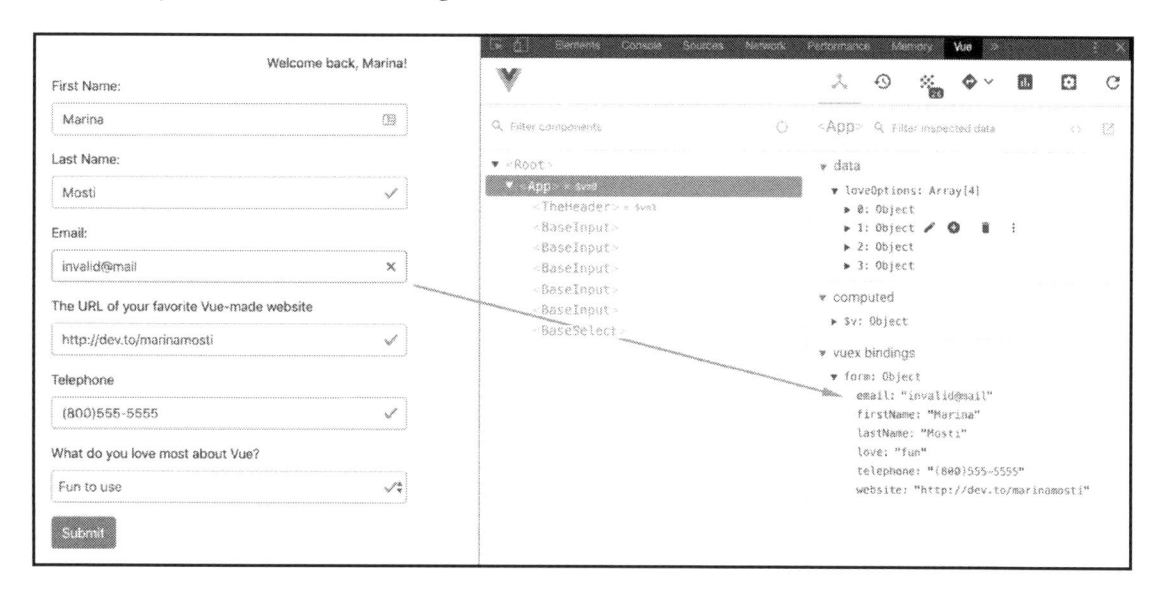

That's it! With these few changes to our application, we have successfully made it so that not only do we have global state ruling over our form, but we also leverage the flexibility and power of Vuelidate to hook into the global state directly.

Summary

In this chapter, you have acquired the necessary skills to set up, create, and use Vuex as a global state pattern and library. You also learned how to hook up Vuelidate with Vuex so that your validation is directly connected to your global state.

In the next chapter, we are going for the final stretch—how to turn all of what we have done, and our form, into a fully schema-driven form.

Creating Schema-Driven Forms

Forms come in different shapes, sizes, and levels of complexity. It is relatively simple to quickly scaffold a login form or a contact form with a few fields, but what happens when you have to take it to the next level and create a completely dynamic form that is driven by an API or schema?

Up until now, we have worked with a relatively simple form that only asks the user for some basic data but everything is hardcoded as a static form. If our mock website wanted to add or remove some fields from the form, we would have to manually make the changes, deploy them to our server, and possibly even adjust the backend to handle the different fields. But what if we wanted to automate this whole process?

In this chapter, we will build an example dynamic form that will be completely powered by an API endpoint. Schema-driven forms are very powerful, as they can be controlled and modified directly by your application's API. That means when something changes in your backend, your form will automatically adjust itself not only on the frontend but also into a self-aware understanding of how to send the dynamic data back to the API.

This chapter will cover the following topics:

- Exploring the starter kit
- Preparing the schema
- Loading the schema and creating a `Renderer` component
- Dynamically binding user data
- Creating a mock API
- Loading the new API into the app
- Translating the API into a working schema

Technical requirements

I will assume that you have either read or understand the concepts viewed in the previous chapters, such as using Axios for HTTP calls and component creation, and have installed on your system as a mock API provider. You can refer to this link for more information: https://mockoon.com/.

To expedite the scaffolding of our app, I have set us up with a starter Vue CLI-3-powered repository with a couple of custom components and a sample static form. You can clone or download it from the following link:

https://github.com/PacktPublishing/Building-Forms-with-Vue.js/tree/master/Chapter07.

Check out the following video to see the code in action:

http://bit.ly/2VMe3eU

Exploring the starter kit

After you clone or download the starter repository, you will find yourself with a Vue CLI 3 project. The first thing to do is to take a look at what we are going to be working with! The repository contains a very simple form with some input fields and a select box. You can find the structure for the form in App.vue. As you can see, we are using two different custom components, BaseInput and BaseSelect. Both of these can be found inside the src/components folder. They both wrap an input and select tag, respectively, and expose some properties that we can use to inject the necessary data into each of them, such as labels and options.

I have taken the liberty of already adding Axios to the project dependencies; you can check out package.json to corroborate. Bootstrap's CSS file for some base classes has been imported inside main.js.

Now that we have a good overview of the project structure, let's go ahead and install the dependencies and run them on our browser. Follow these steps:

1. Go into the Terminal and run the following commands:

   ```
   > npm install
   > npm run serve
   ```

2. After doing this, check out the form on your browser and play around with the fields. There's nothing fancy going on except for the fields being `v-model` bound to the local state in `App.vue`.

The Submit button will only log a message to the console—if you want a refresher on how to send form data to your server, check out `Chapter 2`, *A Form in its Simplest Form*, of this book.

Now that you have an understanding of the starting point of our application, we are going to prepare the demo schema in the next section.

Preparing the schema

Currently, our form (as previously stated) is hardcoded. The first step that is required to start making it a dynamic form is to remove the need to add `BaseInput` or `BaseSelect` directly to our `App.vue` file every time we need to add a new field. This implies that we are going to need to have some sort of organized structure, or schema, to represent what we are trying to accomplish for our form. Since we are using JavaScript, the most logical way to do this is with a JSON object format. This will make it easier later on when we want to take it a step further and have our mock API feed the information directly to our form.

For now, we will use a static schema. Let's create a data folder inside `src`, and inside of it, make a new `schema.json` file. We are going to populate our JSON file with some dummy data. I have chosen, for the sake of an example, to make the top element an object, and each property inside of it will represent one of the fields in our form. Each element will consist of at least a `component` property and a `label` property. In the case of drop-down menus, however, we will also include `options` to populate it.

Creating Schema-Driven Forms

To create the demo schema, add the following data to `schema.json`:

```
{
    "firstName": {
    "component": "BaseInput",
        "label": "First name"
    },
    "lastName": {
        "component": "BaseInput",
        "label": "Last name"
    },
    "favoriteAnimal": {
        "component": "BaseSelect",
        "label": "What's your favorite animal?",
        "options": [
            { "label": "Cat", "value": "cat" },
            { "label": "Dog", "value": "dog" },
            { "label": "Sea Otter", "value": "onlyvalidanswer" }
        ]
    }
}
```

Now that we have a structured schema as a demo of what we want our dynamic form to understand, we can proceed to the next section—where we will load this schema into our application with the help of a `Renderer` component.

Loading the schema and creating a Renderer component

Now that we have a basic schema set up to work with, let's go ahead and load into the application so that we can use it. Later on in this chapter, we are going to create a dummy API that will feed us the data in a slightly different way, and we will transform it on our end to fit our app's requirements.

For now, let's go to `App.vue` and import the JSON. We will start by adding the following `import` statement to the top near the other import statements:

```
import schema from '@/data/schema.json';
```

Now that we have our data available to our application, we need some components to be able to parse this information into the `BaseInput` and `BaseSelect` components. Let's go ahead and create a new file inside the `components` folder, and name it `Renderer.vue`. This component will have a single purpose: to understand our schema and render the correct component to the screen. It will currently have a single property, `element`, which represents each of the elements in our schema. To do so, add the following code to `Renderer.vue`:

```
<template>
  <component
    :is="component"
    v-bind="props"
  />
</template>
<script>
export default {
  props: {
    element: {
      type: Object,
      required: true
    }
  },
  computed: {
    component() {
      const componentName = this.element.component;
      return () => import(`./${componentName}`);
    },
    props() {
      return this.element;
    }
  }
}
</script>
```

There's a couple of important things to note in this component. They are as follows:

- The `element` prop is an object and will be required. This component will not work at all without it. We have two computed properties. The first component takes care of dynamically loading whichever element we need. First, we create a `componentName` constant and assign it to the value of `element.component`, which is where the string name of our component is stored in the schema.

Creating Schema-Driven Forms

- It's important to mention that we are not just adding this `const` for clarity purposes. The way that computed properties work regarding caching *requires* that this `const` exists here since we are returning a function, which will not be inspected for dependencies.
- When this computed property is called by the `<component>` tag for the `:is` an attribute—it will load the component and pass it over. Note that this will only work if the component is globally registered; in any other case, a computed property that requires the correct component would be needed. For further information on dynamic components, check out the official documentation: https://vuejs.org/v2/guide/components-dynamic-async.html.

The second computed property, `props`, will simply pass down the whole element with its properties as `props` to whatever component we are loading using the `v-on` binding. For example, on the `BaseSelect` component, it will pass down the `options` property in our schema to the component so that it can render the correct options. If you are wondering why we are using a computed property instead of just passing the element directly to the `v-on` directive, you are on the right track. Right now, it is definitely not needed, but having it set up in this way to begin with allows us to, later on, add another level of logic or parsing that could be needed for a particular component.

Let's head back to `App.vue`.

We need to import our `Renderer` component and add it to the `template`. We also need to clean up a bit; we no longer need to manually import `BaseInput` or `BaseSelect`, and our form local state will be soon dynamic—so, there's no need to declare it statically, as shown in the following code snippet:

```
<template>
  <div id="app" class="container py-4">
    <div class="row">
      <div class="col-12">
        <form>
          <Renderer
            v-for="(element, name) in schema"
            :key="name"
            :element="element"
          />
          <div class="form-group">
            <button
              @click.prevent="onSubmit"
              type="submit"
              class="btn btn-primary"
            >Submit</button>
          </div>
```

```
            </form>
        </div>
      </div>
    </div>
</template>

<script>
import schema from '@/data/schema.json';
import Renderer from '@/components/Renderer';
export default {
  name: 'app',
  components: { Renderer },
  data() {
    return {
      schema: schema,
      form: {}
    }
  },
  methods: {
    onSubmit() {
      console.log('Submit clicked');
    }
  }
}
</script>
```

Go ahead and run it in the browser and you should see the three inputs that the schema declared in `schema.json`, and the `<select>` should have our three options inside of it. You are going to get a couple of console errors at this point because we haven't worked on our two-way value bindings for our components, and they're set as required. But don't worry, we'll get back to that soon!

Dynamically binding the user's data

What good is any form if we can't use the data that the user inputs? As cool as it is that we can generate these forms dynamically based entirely on a schema, we still need to be able to store these values somehow so that we can later process them as we need. The first step for our form to be able to create two-way bindings is to tell `Renderer.vue` how to handle input events from the dynamic components.

Creating Schema-Driven Forms

Follow these steps:

1. Let's go into `Renderer.vue` and add a `:value` binding, as well as an `@input` listener to the `<component>`:

   ```
   <component
     :is="component"
     v-bind="props"
     :value="value"
     @input="handleComponentInput"
   />
   ```

   Remember that, in order to `v-model` or two-way bind into a custom component, we usually need to pass in a value and listen to input events. In this case, we are going to explicitly listen to input events since our custom components all fire this type of event for two-way bindings.

2. Go ahead and add the new `value` prop to our `Renderer` component:

   ```
   props: {
     element: {
       type: Object,
       required: true
     },
     value: {
       required: true
     }
   }
   ```

   Finally, we need to implement the `handleComponentInput` method. Keep in mind that I have chosen to make it a method instead of just firing the `$emit` directly into the `template` for two reasons. The first one is that I have found it to be a nice practice to more easily write unit tests later on, and second, it allows for more flexibility if we need to write an `if` statement or conditional for a particular component that has specific requirements.

3. Add the new `handleComponentInput` method:

   ```
   methods: {
     handleComponentInput (value) {
       this.$emit('input', value);
     }
   }
   ```

Now that the renderer is ready to two-way bind with `v-model`, let's go back to `App.vue`, where we are implementing it and add the actual binding. We are going to add the `v-model` attribute to `<Renderer>`, and the trick here is that we are going to bind it to `form[name]`. Remember that our schema has a structure where the name of the property is the unique identifier for that field. Open `schema.json` to check it out.

For example, in the first field, `firstName` is the name of the property that holds the first space in the schema object. This property is what we are going to use to bind to so that we can, later on, know which field it represents in our data.

4. Let's add our `v-model` to `<Renderer>` in `App.vue`:

   ```
   <Renderer
     v-for="(element, name) in schema"
     :key="name"
     :element="element"
     v-model="form[name]"
   />
   ```

   Open up your browser and check out your form; if you start filling out the fields and look at your `Vue` development tools, you will see that the bindings are all working correctly. What renderer is doing through the dynamic `v-model` is tying each one of the properties to a property on the form of local data.

5. If you want a quicker way to see this in action without resorting to using the `dev` tools, add this following bit of code to your `<Renderer>` component in `App.vue`:

   ```
   <pre>{{ form }}</pre>
   ```

We are simply going to dump the form into the screen, and use the HTML `<pre>` tag to get some easy formatting. Try going into `schema.json` and adding some new fields. You will see the results on your browser immediately, as renderer will pick up on the changes of the schema and the page will reload by itself (hot reload). With the new schema in place, you will see all of your new fields in place.

We're getting places and fast! In the following section, we're going to prepare yet again for a demo API. In a real application, you are not going to be serving the schema from a file—but probably from a server. Fire up Mockoon, and let's do this!

Creating a mock API

The next step in our demo is to create an actual mock API, which we will then translate into a structure that our renderer understands. Why are we approaching the problem this way? In real work scenarios, it is not uncommon that the backend will not match completely the necessities of the frontend. Perhaps the API was built first, or was made with an earlier version of the frontend in mind that worked in a wildly different way; there are many possibilities, and in this case, we will adjust to an incompatible API to learn how to guard against this.

This approach also ensures that we have a middleman that is going to *translate* and understand the API for our app. If the API were to change for whatever reason, we could safely just change this middleman to adjust for the changes and, in most cases, not even have to touch any of the internal components of the app.

Follow these steps:

1. Start up Mockoon, the app we've been using throughout this book for our dummy API calls. If you haven't yet installed it, you can find the download link here: `https://mockoon.com/`.
2. Make sure the environment is running by clicking on the green play button, and click on the **Add route** button on the top of the second column. On the right-hand screen, we will add some data. Let's start with the path.
3. Under **Route settings**, leave **GET** as the default verb for the route, and go ahead and name the path `/schema`.
4. Go ahead and navigate to the second tab, **Headers**, and set a single header to **Content-Type**: `application-json`. On the plus side, this will give us some nice color coding on the next part.
5. Go back to the first tab, **Response & Body**.
6. Inside the **Body** section, go ahead and copy the following structure. Note that it is not what we had before in our `schema.json` file, but a similar structure that we are going to have to interpret later on. We will even ignore some of the data in there since it won't be of use for our current form—it is not uncommon for APIs to sometimes return data that we don't really use:

```
{
  "fieldCount": 4,
  "fields": [
    {
      "type": "input",
      "id": "firstName",
      "label": "First Name"
```

```
        },
        {
            "type": "input",
            "id": "lastName",
            "label": "Last Name"
        },
        {
            "type": "input",
            "id": "email",
            "label": "Email"
        },
        {
            "type": "singleChoice",
            "label": "What's your favorite animal?",
            "opts": [
                { "label": "Cat", "value": "cat" },
                { "label": "Dog", "value": "dog" },
                { "label": "Sea Otter", "value": "onlyvalidanswer"
                }
            ]
        }
    ]
}
```

Take a good look at the structure of the JSON that is being returned by the API in this case. You will start to see some similarities in how the backend is trying to describe what it needs, and what the renderer on the frontend is expecting to get.

If you are faced with this type of choice in your day-to-day life, you will realize there are two ways we can go about it:

- We can either change the frontend implementation on a component level to adjust to the new API, which in some instances could be what we want.
- Or, we can make a small library or file that will interpret the API for our backend. We are going for this choice for the reasons I have described earlier.

Now that we have our dummy API, we can teach our application how to *translate* this new API format into something that it understands. This part of the process is very important, as you don't want to have to modify your whole application every time there's a change in the backend.

Loading the new API into the app

Right now, if you head into `App.vue`, you will notice we are loading the static schema through an `import` statement, as shown here:

```
import schema from '@/data/schema.json';.
```

This worked very well for us before, as it was a static file, but this time around, we need to make a call to our API endpoint to get the schema for our form. Let's start by removing the import statement; we don't need it anymore and can safely delete it. You can also go into the `data()` properties and set `schema` to a default, which will be an empty object:

```
schema: {},
```

I think that a good place to load our form's schema will be on the created hook for our `App.vue` file. We want to get this done as soon as possible, and we don't really need to manipulate any DOM when it loads, just set the result of the call to the schema's internal property.

Follow these steps:

1. Let's import Axios to the top of our `App.vue` file, near the `Renderer` import, since we are going to use it shortly:

   ```
   import axios from 'axios';
   ```

2. Go ahead and add a newly created hook to our `App.vue` component; inside of it, we will make a simple Axios call to our mock API endpoint. Remember to check on Mockoon to see that it is running:

   ```
   created() {
     axios.get('http://localhost:3000/schema')
     .then(response => {
       this.schema = response.data;
     })
     .catch(error => {
       console.log('Network error', error);
     })
   }
   ```

We are making a call to our new endpoint, `http://localhost:3000/schema`, with the Axios `GET` method. Make sure you check that Mockoon is using the port `3000` for your mock API, or feel free to adjust the URL as needed. Axios calls return a promise—if it fails, we are going to log the error. If the call is successful however, we want to make sure that we capture the whole response and pass down the `data` property of this response to the schema's internal data. It's important to keep in mind that, in this particular case, the response the API is giving us should be the direct JSON schema object. If your API returns a different structure, such as a nested object or array, you will have to adjust accordingly.

Open up your browser and reload the page if needed. It looks like we managed to break the application completely, as was expected. When we assigned the new APIs response to our schema's `data` property, the application tried to load each of the items into the renderer, but it is not prepared to understand this new format of schema that our backend is serving us.

In the next section, we will take a look at how to build a very lean utility library that will allow us to parse this new structure into what the renderer can understand.

Translating the API into a working schema

Now that we have our mock API running, the next step is to create a way for our application to parse or translate this API structure into the schema structure that we had before, and that it understands. If you are curious enough to try to run the application at this point, you will encounter a ton of console errors that yell at you about **prop: type check failed** and `v-model` failing to bind. This is expected at this point.

Go ahead and create a new folder inside `src`; we are going to call it `libraries`. This is not a strict naming convention, so feel free to name it whatever makes more sense to you or your team. Inside this folder, we are going to make a new file called `Api.js`. Our goal for this file is to put all of the code that handles the parsing of the API schema into the app's schema here. This way, we can import whatever we need into our components, and we have a single source of truth regarding the translation of API to schema—if either of these ends change for any reason, we only have to update it here.

Follow these steps:

1. Let's start by adding an entry point; it will be a function called `parse` and will take a single argument: the response from the APIs `schema` endpoint:

   ```
   export const parse = schema => {
     return schema;
   }
   ```

   Right now, we are just going to return the `schema` as is, so we can start with small steps.

2. Go ahead and import this function into `App.vue` at the top:

   ```
   import { parse } from '@/libraries/Api';
   ```

3. Then, inside the created hook, update the `then` block to use the function before we assign it to the state:

   ```
   .then(response => {
     this.schema = parse(response.data);
   })
   ```

   We can go back to `Api.js` now, and we're going to do a basic implementation of this parser. In reality, the complexity of the code here will depend on how much disparity there is between your app's requirements and the APIs structure. Thankfully for us, it only implies a few lines of code.

   Add the following code to `Api.js`:

   ```
   export const parse = schema => {
     const fields = schema['fields'];
     const parsedSchema = {};
     for (let i = 0; i < fields.length; i++) {
       const field = fields[i];
       parsedSchema[field.id] = {
         component: componentForField(field.type),
         label: field.label,
         options: field.opts || null
       }
     }
     return parsedSchema;
   }
   function componentForField(field) {
     switch(field) {
       case 'singleChoice': return 'BaseSelect';
       default: return 'BaseInput';
   ```

            }
        }

Let's break down what is happening here into small chunks:

1. First, we create a constant field, which will just extract the `fields` property out of our API data since it is nested there—we don't really care about the other data it sends.
2. We create a new object, `parsedSchema`, where we will add a property for each of the fields of our form.
3. We loop through each of the items inside of `fields` and create a property for it. In our API schema, the `id` property holds the unique name of the field, so we are going to use that for our property name, `parsedSchema[field.id]`.
4. We assign an inside object to the component property, which is the result of our new `componentForField` function, in which we figure out which component we have to use for each case.
5. For the `options` property, we check whether the `opts` property exists in the API schema or set it as null. It is important to keep in mind that, even if the `BaseInput` component isn't expecting this property, for example, it will not care whether it is there and set to null or undefined.
6. Finally, we return the parsed version of the schema, which our app can use to render the form into its working state.

Go ahead and run it in your browser and behold your schema-driven, API-driven dynamic form!

Summary

Take a moment to give yourself a huge pat on the back. You've made it not only to the end of this chapter but to the end of this book! In this chapter, you have acquired the knowledge and skills to understand the use cases of schema-driven forms, and the ability to create a `Renderer` component to accommodate these cases. You know how to create a library to parse the output from the backend into your own form and how to feed back the form data to the API when needed.

Now, go out, make some dynamic forms, and eat lots of avocados!

Other Books You May Enjoy

If you enjoyed this book, you may be interested in these other books by Packt:

Modern JavaScript Web Development Cookbook
Federico Kereki

ISBN: 978-1-78899-274-9

- Use the latest features of ES8 and learn new ways to code with JavaScript
- Develop server-side services and microservices with Node.js
- Learn to do unit testing and to debug your code
- Build client-side web applications using React and Redux
- Create native mobile applications for Android and iOS with React Native
- Write desktop applications with Electron

Vue.js 2 Design Patterns and Best Practices
Paul Halliday

ISBN: 978-1-78883-979-2

- Understand the theory and patterns of Vue.js
- Build scalable and modular Vue.js applications
- Take advantage of Vuex for reactive state management
- Create Single Page Applications with vue-router
- Use Nuxt for FAST server side rendered Vue applications
- Convert your application to a Progressive Web App (PWA) and add ServiceWorkers, offline support, and more

Leave a review - let other readers know what you think

Please share your thoughts on this book with others by leaving a review on the site that you bought it from. If you purchased the book from Amazon, please leave us an honest review on this book's Amazon page. This is vital so that other potential readers can see and use your unbiased opinion to make purchasing decisions, we can understand what our customers think about our products, and our authors can see your feedback on the title that they have worked with Packt to create. It will only take a few minutes of your time, but is valuable to other potential customers, our authors, and Packt. Thank you!

Index

A
actions
  about 66, 68
  parameters 67
API
  loading, into app 86, 87
  translating, into working schema 87, 89
App.vue file 16
Axios
  about 22
  URL 22
  working with 23, 24

B
BaseSelect element 56
Bootstrap
  about 16
  installing 16, 17
built-in validators
  reference link 49

C
code
  writing 17, 18
components
  form, breaking down into 26, 27, 28, 29
computer
  Vue CLI, installing on 8, 9
custom components
  building, with drop-down input 34, 35, 37, 38, 39
  v-model 29, 30, 31
custom input component
  implementing 31, 32, 33, 34
custom inputs
  enhancing 44, 45
  validation, moving into 52, 53, 54, 55

D
dependencies
  installing 48
drop-down input
  used, for building custom components 34, 35, 37, 38, 39
dynamic components
  reference link 80

F
find method
  reference link 37
form
  about 75
  breaking down, into components 26, 27, 28, 29
  data, submitting of 21, 22

G
global state
  creating 64, 65

I
inputs
  binding, to local state 18, 19, 20

K
key attribute
  reference link 37

L
local state
  inputs, binding to 18, 19, 20

M

mock API endpoint
  creating 61, 62, 63, 64
mock API
  creating 84, 85
Mockoon
  about 23
  download link 84
mutations
  adding, to store 66

P

project
  creating 10
  structure 12
  Vuex, adding to 60, 61
promises
  reference link 24

R

Renderer component
  creating 78, 79, 80, 81

S

schema-driven forms 75
schema
  loading 78, 79, 80, 81
  preparing 77, 78
spread operator
  reference link 71
starter kit
  exploring 76, 77
store
  mutations, adding to 66
style guide and best practices, for naming components
  reference link 27

U

user's data
  binding, dynamically 81, 82, 83

V

v-mask directive 43, 44
v-mask library
  installing 42, 43
v-model
  in custom components 29, 30, 31
  reference link 29
validation rules
  creating 48, 49, 50, 51
validation
  moving, into custom inputs 52, 53, 54, 55
validator
  working 58
Vue CLI
  installing, onto computer 8, 9
Vuelidate
  with Vuex 69, 70, 71, 72
Vuex
  about 59
  adding, to project 60, 61
  URL 59

W

working schema
  API, translating into 87, 88

Printed in Germany
by Amazon Distribution
GmbH, Leipzig